Remembering Bill Neal

Remembering Bill Neal

favorite recipes from a life in cooking

Moreton Neal

FOREWORD BY JOHN T EDGE

The University of North Carolina Press   Chapel Hill & London

Designed by Richard Hendel
Set in Quadraat and Pablo types by Eric M. Brooks
Manufactured in the United States of America

The paper in this book meets the guidelines for permanence and
durability of the Committee on Production Guidelines for Book Longevity
of the Council on Library Resources.

Frontispiece:
In the kitchen at Crook's Corner,
through the courtesy of Gene Hamer and Bill Smith.
(Photograph by Greg Plachta)
Title page:
Bill Neal at the bar at Crook's Corner, 1988.
(Photograph by Richard Fawn)

Library of Congress Cataloging-in-Publication Data
Neal, Moreton.
Remembering Bill Neal: favorite recipes from a life in cooking /
[compiled by] Moreton Neal; foreword by John T Edge.
p. cm.
Includes index.
ISBN 0-8078-2913-7 (cloth: alk. paper)
1. Cookery, American—Southern style. I. Neal, Bill. II. Title.
TX715.2.S68N43   2004
641.5975—dc22   2004009093

08 07 06 05 04   5 4 3 2 1

For Matt, Elliott, and Madeline

Contents

Foreword

Bill Neal's star is ascendant once again. Markers are omnipresent. First editions of his books are fetishized. Paperbacks still sell briskly. Chef-acolytes gather for tribute dinners across the region and beyond. His signature dish of shrimp and grits has claimed its place in the restaurant canon. And benighted souls like me—who never had the chance to taste his cooking or shake his hand—proclaim his name when talk turns to matters of authenticity and Southern *terroir*.

I wasn't there at the moment his star first rose in the sky. (Thanks to Moreton Neal's new book, you will be.) But a couple of years back I made a determined effort to understand what happened when Bill Neal burst forth onto the national restaurant scene. What follows is my distillation of events. Consider it an *amuse-gueule* to Moreton's bounty.

On May 30, 1985, *New York Times* food critic Craig Claiborne rapped at the screen door of a one-bedroom apartment in the university town of Chapel Hill, North Carolina. Bill Neal, the thirty-four-year-old chef at Crook's Corner—a proto-funky bistro with a pink fiberglass pig mounted on the roof, at the prow, like a ship's figurehead—met him at the door and ushered the kingmaker into a narrow galley kitchen. After the two Southerners exchanged obligatory pleasantries, Neal turned his attention to boning quail and shelling shrimp. Claiborne pulled up a stool, plopped his battered typewriter on top of the water heater, and began to peck out a story.

Six weeks later, Neal awoke to a fusillade of phone calls from well-wishers. Claiborne's article declared Neal's cooking to be delectable and his culinary intellect unimpeachable. What's more, Claiborne gave voice to Neal's contention that "the regional dishes of this country are as worthy of preservation as the nation's monuments and architecture."

Claiborne's visit coincided with an early publicity push for *Bill Neal's*

Southern Cooking, scheduled for release that fall by the University of North Carolina Press. The timing was fortuitous. New American cooking was in vogue. Indeed, the canonization of the movement's leaders and the codification of the genre were already well under way.

At the time Claiborne came calling, Bill Neal was not new to the klieg lights of fame. A December 1979 *Fortune* review—written while Neal was the chef at La Résidence—had parroted the view of "several food experts" who considered Neal to be "the most talented young chef in the country." But he had only recently hit his true stride, when, in March 1982, along with partner Gene Hamer, he opened Crook's Corner, refashioning his passion for French cookery into a culinary and cultural exploration of his own backyard.

"Bill was one of the first Southern chefs who had read and traveled widely, who possessed a sophisticated palate and applied that knowledge to a restaurant kitchen," chef Frank Stitt of the Highlands Bar and Grill in Birmingham, Alabama, told me. Like Neal, Stitt opened his restaurant in 1982. "With the publication of Bill's book, and the notice given to the work of Edna Lewis, the South began to earn some respect," said Stitt. "I considered him to be a kindred spirit, a pioneering force in the renaissance of Southern cuisine."

Stitt's sentiments were shared by many of Neal's contemporaries. "When Bill Neal passed away in 1991, I had not yet had the chance to meet him," recalled Louis Osteen, chef-owner of Louis's at Pawleys in South Carolina. "But I sure knew who he was. I knew his books. I knew him to be one of the seminal figures in Southern cuisine. You still hear chefs invoke his name all of the time. It's as if he is still with us."

Curly-headed, with a boyish countenance, Neal was a masterful marketer. He knew how to sell the foods of his native region. He dubbed pimento cheese spread "the pâté of the South." He concocted a traditional Brunswick stew that, in a bow to modern convention, relied on the gamy tang of rabbit rather than squirrel. He tossed plump shrimp atop a mound of stone-ground grits and pronounced the resulting dish worthy of a white tablecloth.

When phoned by newspaper food editors, he gave good copy. He knew the value of context, of culture, of personal recollection. Asked the rote question, What's your favorite food?, Neal was adept at weaving a compelling tale. "Quail is absolutely my favorite food," he told a reporter in 1985. "My father always hunted. I remember reaching into his pockets to get the still-warm birds. Grandma would clean them, Momma would cook them, and we would all eat them." Asked about his favorite fish, Neal would launch into a tale of watching his great-grandfather make catfish stew, taking considerable pains to describe how the old man would nail a fish to a tree and strip the skin from the still-writhing carcass.

When Neal was in his prime, a critical mass of food folk began to build in and around Chapel Hill, recalled Ben Barker, who, along with his wife Karen, owns Magnolia Grill in nearby Durham: "We were fresh out of school at the C.I.A. [Culinary Institute of America], and I had written to Bill with the hope that he would hire us both. He responded, saying that he didn't hire culinary school graduates, and referred us instead to Moreton, who, by that time, was running La Résidence. She hired us in 1982. At the time we arrived, the culinary scene was coming into its own. Edna Lewis was cooking at Fearrington House in nearby Pittsboro. Bill was cooking at Crook's. Even after we arrived, his specter hung in the air at La Résidence. He brought an intellectual rigor to his cooking, a dedication to a depth of flavor that still informs what we do. We still use a spice mix—salt, pepper, nutmeg, and lemon zest—that he developed for cream-based soups. People who don't even know who he is know him by the spices."

In the Barkers' wake came a host of other chefs-to-be. Some, like John Currence, chef-owner of City Grocery in Oxford, Mississippi, were wayward rock-and-rollers in search of a menial job. "I started out bussing tables," recalled Currence, "but it was decided that I lacked the requisite people skills for that job. So I switched to washing dishes and—under Bill's tutelage—worked my way up to kitchen manager. I learned the art of simplicity from Bill. He taught me to take pride in our foods." For Robert Stehling of Hominy Grill in Charleston, South Carolina, a stint in Neal's kitchen opened the door to the possibilities of food. "Bill taught me to cook with a dictionary," said Stehling. "He was a thinker, a reader, and a writer. He was committed to seasonal cooking. When I read glowing reports of Alice Waters in the press, I recognized that under Bill—with Bill—we were doing that too."

Kevin Callahan worked first as a waiter and later as a cook at Crook's. Now he owns Acme Food and Beverage Company, located in Carrboro a few blocks from where Neal lived at the end of his life. "Bill came along at a time when dining out in the South meant a trip to a steak house, a Chinese restaurant, or a country club," said Callahan. "He was the first person I knew of to claim that Southern food, the kind of food served at family reunions, deserved respect. That attitude had an effect on what it meant to work in a restaurant. Bill showed us all that it was worthwhile work. Today we all stand on his shoulders."

Bill Neal passed away in October 1991. He was forty-one. Moreton Neal told me that, at the time, he was in the throes of yet another transformation: "Toward the end of his life, he saw himself as more of a writer than a chef. He was writing for magazines like *Esquire*, and he was under contract with Knopf for a book on Southern vegetables. At this point he had finished three—almost four—books and he was in love with the idea of being a writer." There was a prescience about him, said Moreton. "He knew his work was a harbinger of things to come; he knew that he would not be on this earth too very long."

We are now in the midst of a Neal renaissance. As chefs and writers look back on the regional cuisine boom of the 1980s and try to figure out what happened and why, Bill Neal's name is bandied about with increasing frequency, and a tentative understanding of his legacy is beginning to emerge. "It makes perfect sense to me," said Bill Smith, who took over the kitchen at Crook's Corner two years after Neal's death and has won a reputation of his own by way of such inventive Southern fare as honeysuckle sorbet. "Bill's recipes endure; they still form the backbone of our menu. We serve his hushpuppies, his hoppin' John. The South is evolving; Southern cooking is evolving. Bill wrote it all down at a time when we needed that. He cooked collards when no one deemed them worthy of a fine-dining restaurant. That mattered."

John T Edge

Preface

*He wrote cookbooks that became bibles,
founded restaurants that still live a decade after his death,
and sparked a grits revival that bordered on a renaissance.*
Kathleen Purvis, Charlotte Observer

When Bill Neal died in 1991, he was just hitting his stride as a food writer. The success of his first two cookbooks allowed him to retire from the grueling job of running a restaurant kitchen, and by 1988 he was devoting most of his time to writing. Bill's flair for the written word, his passion for history, and his genius for cooking and gardening promised so much more for his readers. His untimely death surely deprived us of many volumes.

But Bill's influence lives on. The restaurants he founded, Crook's Corner and La Résidence, are still going strong in Chapel Hill. Several of Bill's protégés opened noteworthy restaurants elsewhere in the South using many of his recipes and emulating his special flair. It's hard to find a Southern restaurant these days that does not offer some version of shrimp and grits, the recipe he popularized in his first cookbook. All four of his books—the three cookbooks and *Gardener's Latin*—are still in print, and many of his dishes continue to appear regularly on the menu at Crook's.

Bill grew up in the rural South and is best known for his Southern American cooking, but his instincts were honed as he methodically learned the techniques of French cuisine. For the first ten years of his professional life, both his cooking vernacular and his passion were rooted in a different South—the South of France.

In the introduction to *Bill Neal's Southern Cooking*, he explains the shift: "I had to go abroad to appreciate the mystery of food and its rituals in my native southland. . . . I saw it first in the lives of people whose languages, customs, and culture were foreign, but whose values were mine, before I saw the richness in my, my family's, my region's life."

Bill's new vision crystallized after Craig Claiborne, food editor of the *New York Times*, visited Chapel Hill in 1983 and invited Bill along with him to sample Carolina barbecue joints. Through Claiborne's eyes, Bill began to notice the richness and distinctiveness of Southern American cuisine. Soon after that, he took time off from Crook's and put pen to paper. *Bill Neal's Southern Cooking*, published in 1985, was the result.

Years after the book's publication, Bill explained his mission: "In the preface of the book, I wrote, 'Not long ago I read that to judge from southern cookbooks published in recent times, one would assume beef Stroganoff was a traditional dish. My heart sank.' My rebuttal was to write a small personal book that looked back over three hundred years of pioneer settlement, native displacement, and enslaved importation that created a cuisine unique among the food cultures of the world."

The purpose of this book is less intellectually ambitious, but certainly just as personal. Though Bill is now widely known as a historian and codifier of Southern recipes, his personal repertoire covered a much broader territory. Before the publication of his *Southern Cooking*, and the subsequent reorientation of the cuisine at Crook's, menus there and at La Résidence reflected Bill's "Mediterranean" aesthetic. So closely identified has he been with Southern American food that these recipes have remained, until now, neglected.

In 1999 Frances Gualtieri, who had owned and managed La Résidence since 1992, called to tell me that she and her husband Tom were thinking of putting the restaurant up for sale. (They later changed their minds.) My immediate reaction was, "I need to find our old recipes to pass on to the children before they end up in the garbage!" Most of these recipes, developed by Bill and all of us at La Res, were no longer available on the La Résidence menu, nor could they be found in other local restaurants. Rick Robinson's Mondo Bistro, spiritually kin to the original La Res, had closed by then, leaving a void of good French bistro food on the Chapel Hill side of the Research Triangle. That kind of cooking, to my mind the best in the world, was out of fashion, replaced by a style of cuisine called "fusion," which could mean just about anything. I was determined to save my favorite recipes, the ones I thought of as the standards, to cook for family and friends at home.

During the process of rescuing those faded cards from La Résidence's battle-scarred recipe box, I realized that even the most purely "French" of

Bill and Moreton Neal in the La Résidence kitchen at Fearrington,
April 1976, a few weeks before opening the restaurant.

our dishes were a fusion of local produce and traditional technique. We adapted classic recipes all the time, substituting butter beans for flageolets, green asparagus for white, mountain trout for sole. Our bouillabaisse hadn't an ounce of *loup de mer* or *rouget*; we used North Carolina coastal grouper and snapper instead. And when Bill concocted dishes with Asian flavors (we were not beyond an occasional fusion of cultures ourselves), he would irreverently give them faux French names such as *soupe à la chinoise*.

When I decided to expand this collection to include Crook's Corner recipes, I made a similar discovery. There were dozens of delicious menu items served there, particularly in the early years, that do not fall into the category of "Southern." The white bean soup is Tuscan in character; the chili and enchiladas that sporadically appear on the menu aren't any more Southern than the heart-sinking beef Stroganoff. Orange County farmers deliver fresh fennel, artichokes, and asparagus—decidedly not traditional North Carolina vegetables—to the kitchen door at Crook's. Like Bill Neal, current chef Bill Smith calls his menu "seasonal produce–driven" rather than strictly Southern. Next to hoppin' John, you may, on occasion, find braised leeks. The leeks are grown in Chatham County, so the dish counts as Southern, doesn't it?

The thread that holds these recipes together, particularly the ones that Bill prepared at home, is not at all regional. The collection is eclectic. What these recipes do have in common is a certain style. Whether they came from an old tradition or were the creations of Bill and his staff, or somewhere in between, these dishes are reflections of his personal taste and deserve to be preserved and shared. The collection can be summed up as "what Bill really liked to eat." You will find some surprises here, especially in the "At Home" chapter. Bill's taste could be quite prosaic at times. A mutual friend confided that she was invited to his house for dinner and was shocked that "the great chef" served pepperoni pizza. I've not included that recipe here either. To taste it, you can do as Bill did: call Domino's.

Because this book is meant to be a "best of Bill" collection, I have included hoppin' John, shrimp and grits, chocolate chess pie, and many more classics from Bill Neal's *Southern Cooking, Biscuits, Spoonbread, and Sweet Potato Pie*, and *Good Old Grits*. Recipes for the La Résidence and Crook's chapters were developed from the recipe files of both restaurants, graciously given to me by Frances Gualtieri and Gene Hamer. The "home" recipes came from the sketchy handwritten cookbook Bill and I began after we married, from his Carrboro kitchen files, and from memory. Unfortunately, I never found that beef Stroganoff recipe we enjoyed in graduate school! I think its inclusion here would have made Bill chuckle.

Given his knack for being ahead of the curve, Bill's early death was almost not a surprise. Even in college, he had a premonition that his life would be short. He packed more living into forty-one years than most of us do in twice that many. His fatal illness forced Bill to become all too aware of the meaning of "quality of life" long before most of us give much thought to running out of time on this earth. He lived by the adage "Life is too short to drink bad wine," with all its connotations. In his final years Bill focused his waning energy on his favorite activities: cooking for friends and family, gardening, writing, and drinking excellent wine!

Bill's finely tuned taste buds were discerning to the end. On the night he died, he instructed me to send back his ginger ale to the hospital kitchen. "Something is missing," he insisted. "Tell them it needs just a drop of bitters."

Remembering Bill Neal is a tribute to Bill's talent, his love for food, and his deep commitment to Matt, Elliott, and Madeline Neal, who spent so many happy hours cooking and gardening with their dad. To them, Bill's friends, patrons of his restaurants, fans of his cookbooks, and those of you who just love good cooking, I'd like to say, "Enjoy the feast!"

Acknowledgments

I am grateful to more people than I can name for their help in writing this book, but special thanks are due to the following:

David Perry, editor in chief of UNC Press, for nurturing this project from the beginning.

Paul Betz, project editor at UNC Press, for elbow grease, spit, and polish.

Bill Smith, Gene Hamer, Jean Marie Neal, Maxine Mills, John T Edge, Robert Stehling, John Taylor, Susan Perry, Pat Stronach, Jim and Ellie Ferguson, Sharon Ryan, Nicholas Read, Fred Benton, Frances Gualtieri, and Georgia Kyser for sharing their memories.

Pam Sulser and Steve Levitas, whose generous help with the manuscript and recipe testing were invaluable.

My cooking group—Alice Welsh, Ann Stewart, Mary Hill, and Pat Owens—for recipes, reminiscences, and three decades of good company.

Elizabeth Woodman, Maudy Benz, Sheila Neal, Ellen Virchick, Margaret Skinner, and Archie Copeland for help with editing, typing, and testing.

Tom and Cheri Klein, Ben and Karen Barker, Nancy Brown, Rick Robinson, Barbara Tolley, Jack Haggerty, Cooley Lawrence, Julia Stockton, and many more wonderful cooks who helped Bill develop recipes in the kitchens of both La Résidence and Crook's Corner over the years.

My late friend Carroll Kyser and my late father, Henry Hobbs, whose love and wisdom showed me how to forgive. Without their example, my relationship with Bill Neal would have died with our divorce, and my life would have been the poorer for it.

Matt, Elliott, and Madeline Neal and Erin Maynard, all excellent tasters.

My heart's delight, my husband Drake Maynard, who has tolerated living with the ghost of Bill Neal with grace and humor. Without Drake's bounty of support, both emotional and technological, this project would never have been completed or, for that matter, even begun.

Remembering Bill Neal

La Résidence

APPETIZERS AND SOUPS

Hors d'Oeuvres Variés Platter

Artichokes Basquaise

Artichokes with Tomato Fennel Sauce

Asparagus with Rosemary Mayonnaise

Asparagus and Shrimp Dijonnaise

Beet and Endive Salad

Celeriac Rémoulade

Gnocchi Verdi with 2 Sauces

Leek Gratin

Chicken Liver Mousse

Country Pâté

Pissaladière

Apple Celeriac Soup

Carrot Soup

Mushroom Soup Forestière

Cream of Onion Soup

Onion Soup Lyonnaise

Spring Soup

Winter Soup

CONDIMENTS
Onion Jam
Green Sauce
Ravigote Sauce
Rouille
La Résidence House Vinaigrette
Lemon Vinaigrette

VEGETABLES AND SIDE DISHES
Asparagus with Brown Butter and Capers
Broccoli or Corn Timbales
Grated Carrot Salad
La Res Potatoes
Turned Potatoes
Ratatouille
Timbale of Spinach and Mint with Fresh Tomato Sauce
White Bean Casserole
White Bean Purée
Zucchini Delight

MAIN COURSES
Bouillabaisse
Paella
Mountain Trout à la Bonne Femme
Trout Provençale
Trout Rolls with Ginger-Mushroom Filling
Filet Mignon with Composed Butter

Boeuf en Daube Provençale
Calf's Liver with Avocado
Chicken Stuffed with Spinach and Cheese
Chicken with 40 Cloves of Garlic
Duck with Red Wine and Shallots
Duck Breasts with Sauce Carroll
Cassoulet
Lamb Curry
Grilled Leg of Lamb
Braised Pork with Bourbon and Prunes
Sweetbreads with Capers and Brown Butter
Sweetbreads Ecossaise
Veal Chops Italienne
Osso Bucco
Veal Kidneys with Mushrooms

DESSERTS

Queen of Sheba Cake
Tarte Tatin
Kalouga
Chocolate Roulade
Walnut Roulade
Crème Anglaise
Honey Chocolate Sauce
Espresso Ice Cream
Fig Ice Cream with Port
Galliano Chocolate-Chunk Ice Cream

Ginger Ice Cream
Honey Thyme Ice Cream
Caramel Mousse
Chocolate Mousse
Lemon Mousse
Grand Marnier Sabayon
Blackberry Sorbet
Passion Fruit Sorbet
Fresh Fruit with Mint and Lillet
Brown-Edged Wafers

BEVERAGES
Cocktail La Res
French 75
La Résidence Coffee Blend

La Résidence was one of the first gourmet restaurants
to come on the scene, and people in the area who had traveled
to other parts of the country responded enthusiastically.
The Neals really elevated the appreciation of fine food
in the Triangle.
Marilyn Spencer, Raleigh News and Observer

*B*ill Neal and I first bumped into each other, auspiciously enough, in French class when we were both students at Duke. He was hard to miss in the baggy red and yellow Hawaiian bathing suit he wore to every class—a ploy to catch my attention, he later claimed. It worked brilliantly! After we started dating, we discovered that cooking was a common interest. Almost from the beginning of our relationship, Bill and I whipped up dishes together in my dormitory's crudely equipped kitchen. We also loved to dine out, exploring the local culinary scene. But it wasn't until after we graduated and married that the restaurant bug bit us.

Bill was first introduced to restaurant work during his junior year at Duke. To earn a little pocket money, he hitchhiked from campus to his first serving job at the Country Squire Restaurant between Chapel Hill and Durham. The popular steak house exposed that country boy to the world of college town "fine dining." The Squire's guests sipped Mateus rosé and Taylor cold duck as they consumed fat wedges of iceberg lettuce slathered in sinfully thick blue cheese dressing. After the salad course, not just baked but "twice baked" potatoes appeared next to huge slabs of beef, all served on tables set with blue-and-white-checked tablecloths and napkins to match. This was a far cry from Red Bridges Barbecue in Shelby, Bill's family's favorite supper destination.

It didn't take long for Bill to notice that a waiter's personality could enhance the customers' dining experience and that the "charm factor" made a big difference in the amount of a waiter's earnings. Not surprisingly, Bill's tips were huge.

The two of us enjoyed spending his tip money on our own Mateus at the legendary Danziger family's flagship restaurant in Chapel Hill, the Villa Teo, our very favorite dining spot. This eccentric Franklin Street edifice offered the closest thing to French cuisine, then called "Continental," in these parts. We had no problem coming up with special occasions to justify indulging ourselves there, including our engagement.

During school vacations we visited my hometown in Mississippi, just up the road from the eating capital of the South. At 6:30 A.M. we would hop on the Panama Limited for New Orleans, arriving just in time for breakfast at Brennan's. Lunch at Galatoire's and early supper at Antoine's or Arnaud's rounded out the day. On the train ride back home, we happily digested and reflected on all that good eating. In our experience, the best Southern restaurants were actually French Creole. The menus were written in French, the waiters spoke French, and the food—French with a dash of Tabasco! Our standards and our cooking aspirations were based on the cuisine of New Orleans. Our culinary bible was the 1901 edition of the The Picayune's Creole Cook Book, still the ultimate collection of New Orleans's classic recipes.

A few years later, after we catered our way through graduate school, we abandoned academia for cooking. Bill dreamed of studying at the Cordon Bleu in Paris, but the reality of our meager bank account interfered. Instead, he entered the back door of the Villa Teo in the role of apprentice cook. Two years at the Country Squire had already taught him that restaurant work is a lot like show business: hours of preparation and hard work to be followed by an ostensibly effortless presentation. Pleasing an audience with a superb meal was right up Bill's alley. The Villa's exotic ambience appealed to Bill's desire for glamour, and the "demimonde" of a college-town restaurant kitchen teeming with highly educated eccentrics intrigued him. He was in a fertile creative atmosphere at the Villa and absorbed the lessons of a professional kitchen like a sponge.

Within a year, Bibi Danziger recognized Bill's promise and promoted him to the position of chef de cuisine, replacing his mentor, departing chef Henry Schliff. In the Villa's kitchen, Bill had discovered his true calling. By then I was cooking at Hope Valley Country Club, absorbing the lessons of an actual French chef, Jacques Condoret, but I soon followed Bill to the Villa as pastry cook.

In 1975 we decided the time was ripe to ride the wave of the fine-dining trend of the '70s and open our own place. Our vision was a place where, in the words of Alice Waters, who had just begun her own food revolution at Chez Panisse, "coming to [our] restaurant would be like going to dinner at the home of a friend who really knows how to cook." But finding the appropriate space in Chapel Hill proved harder than we bargained for. We had just about given up our search and considered relocating to another city, when R. B. Fitch, husband of our cooking buddy Jenny, called us about a building in Chatham County, south of Chapel Hill. As soon as we glimpsed the main house at Jesse Fearrington's dairy farm, now the burgeoning Fearrington Village, we fell in love with it, signed the lease, and moved right in.

A week before the restaurant opened, it was still unnamed. Bill and I, with nary a drop of French blood in our veins, had been reluctant to give it a name that would imply that we were French. A newspaper reporter nudged us to make a decision. We invited her to lunch along with a visiting French friend, as well as Georgia Kyser and her daughter Carroll, who were both helping us with the decor. At the table, these ladies dazzled us with tales of their annual summer visits to Provence. Under the spell of the Kysers' nostalgia, we settled on the name of their beloved pension in Saint Paul de Vence, a spellbinding little village that had also captivated us when we were there. The reporter's ensuing article committed us to the name "La Résidence," soon to be shortened to "La Res" by our regular patrons.

Bill and I were so innocent regarding the practical matters of running a restaurant that failing never even entered our minds, at least not his. His confidence swept me away, and we proceeded to run the place "by ear." Bill dazzled his staff and patrons alike, and they loved being a part of the experiment.

Bill Smith, who eventually became chef at La Résidence and now runs the kitchen at Crook's Corner, described the early days working in the kitchen of La Res: "Bill thought of the kitchen as a laboratory where creative possibilities were endless. There was a pied piper quality about him that was very attractive. In Bill's kitchen I learned something besides cooking. I learned that you don't have to be conventional about anything."

Jim Ferguson, initiator of the culinary history program at the University of North Carolina at Chapel Hill, recalled: "What you two did out there was both cutting edge and charmingly naive. For me it was a touchstone to France, an acknowledgment that there is a season for things and a 'right way' to cook." Jim echoes Bill Smith in describing La Res as a laboratory, "a real attempt to develop a sense of what's important about food and about a way of life. No one had done anything like that around here, and there were enough people in tune with that attitude who wanted to support the effort."

Another of the first patrons and later our partner, Pat Stronach, adds: "Bill was enthusiastic, charismatic, and most definitely a performer. He was the first person we knew to bring food as a lifestyle to the Triangle. It felt neat, and really chic, to be a part of that."

Not everyone's idea of a good time is the same, however, and occasionally we failed to please. Our floor manager for years, Susan Perry, reminded me of the time a difficult group of guests demanded to speak to the owner. When Bill appeared at the table, they threatened to walk out. Without missing a beat, Bill replied, "It would be our greatest pleasure." Even when offending, Bill had tremendous flair!

After two years in Chatham County, La Résidence began to suffer growing pains, and being at the restaurant twenty-four hours a day was beginning to take its toll on our family life. In 1978 we moved the restaurant to an old house on West Rosemary Street in Chapel Hill. Everything expanded: the volume of guests, the menu items, the hours worked, the payroll, our family.

Those halcyon days out in Chatham County were over, but there were compensations. No longer was the restaurant a mom-and-pop operation. Out of necessity Bill became, once more, a teacher. Intelligent, imaginative people, mostly graduate students, were attracted to the creative atmosphere at La Res. Bill, almost a cult figure by then, taught these students French technique and inspired them with his passion for excellence. In return, the staff contributed ideas and recipes that reenergized us and enhanced the restaurant. Every week the entire staff was invited to a potluck lunch, with the aim of trying out new dishes. Many of these ended up on the menu.

Looking to describe Bill's special magic, several friends used the same words: "seductive," "unconventional," "a sense of abandon . . . he lived as if there were no tomorrow." As you can imagine, these very qualities made up a recipe for marital disaster. Bill and I ended our marital and business partnership in 1982, but our friendship (after a brief, tempestuous hiatus) survived.

I continued to manage the restaurant with the invaluable help of Cheri Klein and, later, Bill Smith, both protégés of Bill. Along the way, Nancy Brown, Ben and Karen Barker, Rick Robinson, and many other talented souls each added their own touch, but La Res continued in its original style—French country cuisine—and spirit until Smith and I both left in 1992.

New owners Tom and Frances Gualtieri shifted directions. Incoming chef Devon Mills brought an end to an era with his lighter "new American" fare. The Gualtieris still run the restaurant. As I write, an innovative new talent, Graham Heaton, is establishing his own reputation at La Res, and it continues to be a popular nightspot in downtown Chapel Hill.

There is just one recipe that has survived all these changes and still appears nightly on the menu—just about everybody's favorite chocolate cake: Kalouga!

The recipes in this chapter were served at La Résidence from 1976 to 1992. Some can be called "original," though Bill would be the first to admit, as his friend Hoppin' John Taylor reminded me, that "there's nothing new under the sun." Others were contributed by staff members, and still others were adapted from his library of frayed, food-spotted cookbooks by the cooks he most admired: Elizabeth David, Richard Olney, Lydie Marshall, the Troisgros brothers, Judith Olney, Marcella Hazan, Roger Verge, Simone Beck, Madeline Kamman, Jacques Pépin, and, of course, Julia Child.

Bon appétit!

A NOTE ABOUT THE RECIPES

I have adapted these recipes for use in an average home kitchen equipped with what I consider to be basics: good quality nonreactive (stainless steel or other nonaluminum) pots and pans, sharp knives, a food processor, a blender, nonreactive mixing bowls, and a medium-duty mixer (hand-held or stationary).

Few of the recipe cards used at La Résidence included exact amounts. For "a ton," "a bunch," "a million," or "a handful," I have substituted more conventional and exact terms: a tablespoon (T.), a cup (c.), and so on. As for "a pinch," you are on your own!

We emphasized using the freshest possible produce, herbs, meat, and fish, and for best results I suggest you do the same. I have indicated when a dried, frozen, or canned substitute would be appropriate.

As is customary in France, at La Résidence we used unsalted butter—the fresher, the better. (At home we used salted butter, as most Southerners still do.)

We used kosher salt and freshly ground pepper. If a good sea salt is available to you, by all means use it. For purely cosmetic reasons, Bill preferred white pepper when making pale-colored dishes. In such recipes, though, feel free to use the more flavorful black pepper. All pepper should be freshly ground.

Use large-sized eggs unless otherwise indicated.

Our standard brand of chocolate was Peterson's, a rich Dutch import. Substitute Ghirardelli or another top-quality chocolate.

Always use common sense when putting together these dishes, and try not to be too literal. For instance, when making the recipe called "chicken with 40 cloves of garlic," feel free to use either fewer large or more small cloves than called for without feeling compelled to change the name of the recipe!

No matter how good a recipe is, adjustments will have to be made according to the varying qualities of the ingredients you have at hand. Add a pinch of sugar or salt, a drop of lemon juice, a dash of Tabasco, and so on when necessary. Certainly Bill would agree that if there is a secret to good cooking it is "taste as you go along."

APPETIZERS AND SOUPS

Hors d'Oeuvres Variés Platter

Nostalgia compels me to include the most popular menu item at La Res. For those who had a hard time choosing, we always offered a sampler of most of the appetizers available on any given evening—our own "pupu platter." Four or five of the following dishes were presented on a plate—an adventure in tasting.

The recipe for each dish is included in this chapter.

artichokes Basquaise or with tomato fennel sauce
grated carrot salad
celeriac rémoulade
asparagus and shrimp Dijonnaise
country pâté or chicken liver mousse
onion jam
ratatouille
assorted olives and halved hard-boiled eggs with an anchovy placed on each

Arrange several of these appetizers attractively on a large platter and serve cold or at room temperature, garnished with the olives and hard-boiled eggs.

Artichokes Basquaise

Our first-course menu almost always included an artichoke dish. This was one of the best.

Makes 4 large or 8 small servings

4 artichokes
1 lemon, cut in half
Salt and pepper
1/2 lb. bacon
1/2 c. olive oil
2 stalks celery, chopped finely
1 small green pepper, chopped finely
1/2 yellow pepper, chopped finely
1/2 red pepper, chopped finely
2 cloves garlic, minced
6 scallions, chopped finely
zest and juice of 1 lemon

salt and pepper to taste
2 T. chopped parsley

Cut off the top inch or so of each artichoke. (A serrated knife works best.) Slice off the stem at the point where it joins the bottom of the artichoke. With kitchen shears or scissors, cut the tip of each artichoke leaf off evenly about an inch down from the pointy tip, leaving the circle of leaves about 1 1/2 inches high around the choke. Rub the artichokes all over with the cut lemon to prevent discoloration. Squeeze the rest of the lemon juice into a large pot of boiling water and then add the lemon halves to the pot and season with salt and pepper. Add the artichokes and cover with a folded kitchen towel and a small plate to keep submerged. Simmer for 30 minutes or until the heart is tender. (When the artichoke is done, the outer leaves should pull off without difficulty and you should be able to insert a small knife easily into the bottom.)

While the artichokes are cooking, prepare the sauce.

Fry the bacon in a heavy sauté pan until crisp and brown. Drain on paper towels, then chop into very small pieces.

Pour off all but 2 T. bacon grease in the pan, add 2 T. of the olive oil, and sauté the celery, peppers, scallions, and garlic on medium heat until soft but not browned. Remove from heat and let cool. Add lemon zest and juice, salt and pepper, parsley, bacon, and the remaining olive oil.

When the artichokes are cooked, run cold water over them until they are cool enough to handle. Turn upside down on paper towels and drain well.

Carefully scoop out each choke with a spoon, keeping the surrounding leaves and the heart intact.

Turn each artichoke upside down and, with a very sharp knife, slice in half from bottom to top.

On each plate place 1 or 2 of the halves, cut-side up. Just before serving, give the sauce a good stir to mix the ingredients, and spoon a liberal amount of sauce on each artichoke half.

Artichokes with Tomato Fennel Sauce

A make-ahead Mediterranean appetizer from the summer menu. The sauce is equally good served warm or chilled.

Makes 3 large or 6 small servings

3 cooked artichokes, choke removed and sliced in half from bottom to top
(see artichokes Basquaise, page 11)
1 small onion, chopped finely
5 cloves garlic, minced
1/2 fennel bulb, chopped
1 14-oz. can tomatoes, seeded and crushed, with liquid
1 1/2 t. fennel seeds
3 bay leaves
1 1/2 T. capers
salt and pepper

Sauté onion, garlic, and fennel in olive oil until soft but not brown. Add tomatoes with liquid, fennel seeds, and bay leaves. Simmer for 5 minutes longer.

Remove from heat and stir in the capers. Add salt and pepper to taste. Remove the bay leaves.

Place each artichoke half on a plate, cut-side up. Pour sauce over the top and around the sides immediately before serving.

Asparagus with Rosemary Mayonnaise

Asparagus was available for only a few weeks in early spring back in the 1970s. Since then, North Carolina farmers have learned how to stagger the crop and extend the growing season, but any time of year this mayonnaise complements other vegetables such as broccoli and cold poached fish or chicken.

1 lb. fresh asparagus
1 T. Dijon mustard
2 raw egg yolks
3/4 c. olive oil
3/4 c. walnut oil (additional olive oil or canola oil can be substituted
if walnut oil is not available)
2 T. lemon juice
salt and pepper to taste
1 T. fresh rosemary, chopped finely

To prepare asparagus for cooking, hold each asparagus with both hands—one at the tip, the other at the bottom end. Bend the stalk until it breaks naturally (the breaking point should be a couple of inches from the bottom). Discard the tough bottom ends.

In a saucepan, bring enough salted water to boil to cover the asparagus. Cook the vegetables in the water for 2 to 5 minutes (depending on the thickness of stalks) until they are fairly soft but still bright green.

Remove the stalks immediately from the hot water and immerse in ice water to stop the cooking. Drain well.

Combine the mustard and egg yolks in a blender or food processor. Blend or pulse for a couple of seconds before adding, in a very thin stream, the combined oils. About halfway through the addition of the oil, add the lemon juice to lighten the mayonnaise. Continue blending as you add the remainder of the oils until the mayonnaise is thick and will not incorporate any more (the oil may pool on top of the emulsified sauce). If this happens before you use all the oil, just discontinue pouring and reserve the extra oil for another use. Season with salt and pepper. Stir in the rosemary and chill the sauce until ready to serve. (This mayonnaise can be kept for up to a week in the refrigerator.)

Arrange the asparagus in a fan shape on a plate. Spoon the mayonnaise on top.

Asparagus and Shrimp Dijonnaise

On a visit to Southern France in the mid-1970s, Bill and I were guests of a couple who, though not much older, were light years ahead of us in sophistication. At their restored apartment in the quaint village of Maillane, we were served an impressive 7-course dinner. Between each course all the guests danced to soft jazz. Bill and I, our college hippie phase not too far behind us, truly thought we'd died and gone to heaven, or at least been initiated properly into adulthood, suddenly a seductive and promising prospect.

One of the most memorable of the courses served that evening was this very simple asparagus dish, eaten in the French style—picking up the stem end of the vegetable, dipping the tip into the sauce, and popping it into the mouth.

We began serving asparagus Dijonnaise as a first course each spring after the restaurant opened, and later added shrimp to respond to requests for a more substantial appetizer.

Dijonnaise sauce is wonderful with other cold vegetables, such as artichokes and green beans, and with other shellfish. Refrigerated, it keeps up to 2 weeks.

Serves 4

3/4 lb. large fresh shrimp in shells
1 qt. water
2 t. salt
8 black peppercorns
1-inch strip of lemon zest
1 small onion, halved
2 raw egg yolks
2 T. coarse ground mustard (e.g., Pommery)
2 T. Dijon mustard
1 large or 2 small cloves garlic, minced
1/2 t. salt
1 1/2 c. good-quality extra virgin olive oil
(canola oil can be substituted for half the olive oil)

4 drops Tabasco sauce
2 T. lemon juice
1 lb. chilled cooked asparagus (see preceding recipe)
2 T. chopped parsley

In a medium saucepan, bring the water to a boil with the 2 t. salt, pepper-corns, lemon zest, and halved onion. Add the shrimp. Boil for 2 minutes or until shrimp become pink and opaque. Immediately remove from heat and drain shrimp in a colander. Place in a bowl covered with water and ice. When the shrimp are cool, drain off the water. Peel and devein the shrimp. Store in the refrigerator until ready to serve.

Place the egg yolks, mustards, garlic, salt, and Tabasco in a blender. With the blender running, pour the oil into the blender in a very thin stream. About halfway through the addition of the oil, add the lemon juice to lighten the sauce. Continue adding the remainder of the oil until the sauce becomes quite thick. When the oil pools on top of the emulsified sauce, stop the blender. Store in the refrigerator until ready for use.

Arrange the asparagus and shrimp on a salad plate. Drizzle with Dijon-naise sauce and garnish with parsley.

Beet and Endive Salad

Sometimes called "winter salad," this colorful dish appeared on the menu at both Crook's and La Résidence. Bill didn't live to see golden beets become available, but if you can get them, use them along with the red beets for a spectacular effect.

Serves 4

4 medium beets
2 heads Belgian endive
1/2–1 c. vinaigrette made with half walnut oil, half olive oil
(see La Résidence house vinaigrette, page 36)
6 T. chopped fresh parsley
1/2 c. walnuts, toasted and chopped coarsely
1/2 c. crumbled fresh goat cheese

Preheat oven to 400°. Wash the beets and place them in a baking dish with a little water. Cover the dish tightly with aluminum foil and roast the beets until they are tender when pierced with a sharp knife, about 45 minutes. When the beets have cooled, peel them, slice them into thin strips (julienne), and toss with a little vinaigrette.

Slice the Belgian endive crosswise into thin slices (chiffonade). In a glass or wooden bowl, toss the endive with vinaigrette and chopped parsley. Pile the endive onto serving plates. Arrange julienned beets over the endive, taking care not to stain the endive red.

Sprinkle the walnuts and goat cheese over the salad. Add a little more vinaigrette and serve immediately.

Celeriac Rémoulade

Celeriac, a vegetable common in Southern France, is not likely to be found in the average North Carolina Food Lion. But if you happen to run into it in a gourmet grocery, this simple recipe is a good way to get to know one of Bill's favorite vegetables. Commonly called celery root, it is actually a different vegetable than our familiar celery, though celery can be substituted in some recipes (for example, apple celeriac soup). This dish, however, requires the real thing. Bill introduced celeriac rémoulade, a simple side dish prevalent in Provençal bistros, as part of our hors d'oeuvres variés platter. It also makes an excellent accompaniment to country pâté.

Serves 4 to 6

1 large celery root (or 2 of medium size)
2 t. salt
1 T. lemon juice
1/4 c. Dijon mustard
3 T. boiling water
2 T. white wine vinegar
salt and pepper to taste
1/2 c. olive oil
1/2–1 c. matchstick-sized strips of ham (optional)

Trim the top and bottom off the celery root and peel, being sure to remove all brown spots. Cut the celery root into very thin strips, about 2 inches long (julienne). (Note: You can julienne the celery root using the grating blade of a food processor. For best results, cut the celery root in half and place it, cut-side down, in the large feed tube of the processor.) Toss the celery root with lemon juice and salt. Let sit for 30 minutes. Rinse with cold water, then drain, dry thoroughly in a kitchen towel, and reserve in a mixing or serving bowl.

Add the mustard to a warm bowl. Slowly whisk in the water in a steady stream. Stir in the vinegar and season with salt and pepper. Gradually beat in the oil to make a creamy mayonnaise-style sauce.

Add half of the sauce to the celery root and toss gently to combine. Add more sauce if needed, but do not overdress. (Any leftover sauce can be used as a salad dressing or marinade.) For a more substantial appetizer, stir in 1/2 c. or more ham. Allow the salad to marinate for at least an hour before serving.

Gnocchi Verdi with 2 Sauces

Every once in a while Bill, inspired by Marcella Hazan, made a gastronomic detour into Italy. Gnocchi verdi was a big hit as a first course and remained on the menu for years. Unlike most gnocchi, usually made from potatoes and prone to chewiness, these delicate dumplings almost melt in your mouth.

We served the gnocchi covered first in béchamel sauce and then topped with a tomato sauce sprinkled with freshly grated Parmesan cheese.

Serves 4 to 6

2 T. butter
1/4 c. minced onion
2 cloves garlic, minced
1/4 c. finely chopped pancetta or ham
1 package frozen spinach, thawed and well drained
7 1/2 oz. ricotta cheese

1 c. flour
2 egg yolks, beaten
1/2 t. salt
1 1/2 c. freshly grated Parmesan cheese
1/4 t. freshly grated nutmeg
béchamel sauce (recipe follows)
tomato sauce (recipe follows)

Sauté the onion and garlic in butter over medium heat for 2 minutes. Add the ham and spinach, stir to combine, and continue cooking for 5 minutes. Remove the spinach mixture with a slotted spoon to a large mixing bowl. Add the ricotta and 2/3 c. of the flour, mixing thoroughly. Mix in the egg yolks, 1 c. of the Parmesan cheese, salt, and nutmeg until well combined. (The mixture can be stored at this point, covered and refrigerated, for a day or two.)

When ready to cook the gnocchi, bring a large pot of water to a boil. Have the remaining flour available in a small bowl. While the water is heating, begin forming the gnocchi. Using a spoon, scoop up about a tablespoon of the gnocchi mixture, dip it lightly in the flour, and then form it into a ball about 1 1/2 inches in diameter. Place the ball on a cookie sheet covered with wax paper. Continue forming the gnocchi until you have used all the mixture (or you can keep the mixture covered and refrigerated for several days).

When the water reaches the boil, using a slotted spoon place 5 or 6 gnocchi in the water and cook until they begin to float to the surface, about 3 minutes. Remove from the water with the slotted spoon and place in a large shallow baking dish or small individual gratin dishes, lightly buttered. Continue cooking the remainder of the gnocchi in this fashion.

Make the béchamel sauce as described below and pour it generously on top of the gnocchi. Cover with plastic wrap and refrigerate while making tomato sauce as described below.

At this point the gnocchi can be refrigerated for several hours, without the tomato sauce, before serving. When ready to serve, preheat oven to 400°. Spoon tomato sauce on top of the béchamel sauce and gnocchi, sprinkle with the remaining Parmesan, and bake until bubbling hot and the cheese is melted, about 15 to 30 minutes, depending on the size of the pan used. Serve immediately.

BÉCHAMEL SAUCE

4 T. butter
3 T. flour
2 c. warmed milk
1/4 t. salt

In a heavy saucepan melt the butter over medium heat. Add the flour all at once, stirring constantly for 2 minutes, careful not to let the flour color.

Remove the pan from heat and add milk, a little at a time, stirring or whisking to incorporate the milk into the flour mixture smoothly. Place the pot back on medium-low heat and cook, stirring until the sauce thickens. Simmer and stir for 3 minutes longer. Remove from heat.

TOMATO SAUCE

6 T. butter
4 T. minced onion
2 T. minced carrot
3 T. minced celery
2 1/2 c. canned tomatoes, including juice
2 t. salt
pinch of sugar

In a heavy, nonreactive saucepan, sauté the onion, carrot, and celery in the butter for a few minutes. Add the tomatoes and juice, salt, and sugar and simmer over very low heat for 1 hour, stirring frequently.

Leek Gratin

Like other members of the onion family, leeks usually play a supporting role in a recipe. In this case the elegant vegetable is the star of the show.

Serves 4

8 small leeks
2 c. béchamel sauce (page 20, above)

LA RÉSIDENCE

8 thin slices of ham (Westphalian, Black Forest, or other high-quality baked ham)
1 c. grated Gruyère, Emmenthaler, or other Swiss-type cheese
1/2 c. grated Parmesan cheese

Trim the leeks, cutting off the green part. Rinse well, making sure to get out any grit. Bring a pot of salted water to a boil, add the leeks, and simmer uncovered until just tender enough to cut with a dinner knife, about 25 to 30 minutes. Drain the leeks and cool in ice water.

Preheat oven to 375°. In a shallow casserole, place a thin layer of béchamel sauce. Remove the leeks from the ice bath and dry with paper towels. Wrap each leek in a ham slice and place on top of the sauce in the casserole. Top with more béchamel and sprinkle with the cheeses.

Bake for about 15 to 25 minutes or until bubbly and golden on top.

Chicken Liver Mousse

Long before she wrote cookbooks and became restaurant critic for the *Washington Times*, Judith Olney made quite a name for herself in Chapel Hill. Bill was a graduate student when Carroll Kyser, manager of a local kitchenware shop, introduced him to Judy, as she was still known back in the early 1970s. Judy had arrived in town fresh from Provence after studying cooking technique with her brother-in-law, cookbook writer Richard Olney. Carroll persuaded her to teach cooking lessons at her shop, Danziger Design. Dazzled by Judy's beauty, glamour, and skills, Bill was the first to sign up.

As we became friendly with Judy and her husband, we were invited to dine at their house. We considered their home with its country French furnishings to be the very definition of casual elegance, a quality we hoped to absorb just by being there. The first time we encountered chicken liver mousse was at the Olneys' home kitchen. In Judy's hands these humble innards became food for the gods.

A few years later when La Résidence opened, we served a small tureen of chicken liver mousse along with the crunchy French bread placed on every table.

1 1/2 c. butter, softened to room temperature
1 c. chopped onions or shallots
1 lb. chicken livers
2 T. Dijon mustard
3 T. brandy or cognac
pinch of nutmeg
salt and pepper to taste
chopped parsley
French bread or crackers

Sauté the onions in 1/4 c. of the butter over medium heat until translucent. Add chicken livers to the onions and sauté until they are cooked through but not overdone, about 5 to 8 minutes. Remove from heat and cool to room temperature.

Put in a food processor the onions, livers, mustard, brandy, and seasonings. Process the mixture until thoroughly puréed. Add the remaining 1 1/4 c. softened butter in fourths, pulsing briefly after each addition. Spoon the mousse into an attractive small tureen or into ramekins and chill until solid (at least an hour) before serving. Sprinkle with chopped parsley if desired, and serve with sliced French bread or crackers.

Country Pâté

Nothing is more French than country pâté, and it was a regular feature at La Res from day one. Bill never made it quite the same way twice. Even though I provide very specific details in this recipe, feel free to improvise. The carrots and beans used in this version make a decorative pattern when the pâté is sliced. We used to get the traditional lard leaves—thinly sliced unsalted fatback for lining the terrine—from Cliff's Meat Market in Carrboro. They're virtually impossible to find now, so I've substituted bacon in this recipe. You can also use salted fatback that has been rinsed in cold water. This dish should be made at least 2 days in advance of serving.

The recipe calls for using a sizable terrine or loaf pan, but there will still be leftover meat, which can be baked in a small pan or in individual ramekins.

Serves 12 to 16

3 shallots, chopped finely
3 cloves garlic, minced
2 T. butter
4 medium carrots, peeled
15 green beans, ends removed
1 lb. chicken or duck livers
1 1/4 lbs. ground pork shoulder
1 1/4 lbs. ground pork fat
10 oz. frozen spinach, thawed, well drained, and chopped
1 T. salt
1 t. pepper
1/2 t. allspice
1/4 t. dried thyme
1/4 t. dried basil
1/4 c. Madeira
1/4 c. cognac
1 egg, lightly beaten
3/4 lb. bacon
3 bay leaves
Niçoise olives, cornichons
Dijon or grainy mustard
fresh baguette

Sauté the shallots and garlic in the butter over medium heat until soft but not brown, about 3 minutes. Reserve.

Rinse the livers, remove any excess fat, and pat dry with paper towels. Purée in a food processor until liquefied. Combine the puréed liver in a large mixing bowl with the ground pork shoulder and pork fat. Mix in the spinach, seasonings, Madeira, and cognac until all of the ingredients are well combined. If time permits, you can let the mixture marinate, covered and refrigerated, for several hours or several days.

When you are ready to cook the pâté, preheat oven to 350°. Cut the carrots in half and then slice them into thin strips (julienne). Braise the carrots and green beans in lightly salted simmering water until just tender, about 5 minutes. Drain, immerse in ice water, and reserve.

To taste the pâté for seasoning, make a small patty from the mixture and fry over medium heat a couple of minutes on each side, until just done. Taste the cooked pâté and then adjust the seasoning of the mixture to your liking. Add the beaten egg to the mixture and stir to combine. Drain the carrots and beans and pat dry with paper towels.

Line a 12 x 4 1/2-inch terrine (or a 9 1/2 x 5-inch loaf pan) with the bacon, pressing the bacon into the pan as you go. Place the strips horizontally in the pan so that they cover the bottom and both sides with a little overhang. Cut pieces for lining the end, with several inches of overhang. The bacon strips should be touching one another so that the filling will be sealed within. Spread some of the pâté mixture in the bottom of the terrine; then arrange the beans lengthwise in the pan and press into the mixture. Cover the beans with some more of the pâté mixture and then press the carrot strips into the mixture. Add the remainder of the mixture until the terrine is full. Cover the top of the pâté with several additional strips of bacon as needed and fold the overhanging pieces so that the mixture is fully covered. Place the bay leaves on top of the sealed pâté and cover the terrine tightly with aluminum foil. Gently tap the terrine on the countertop to ensure that the mixture is evenly distributed in the pan.

Place the terrine in a baking dish or pan and fill the pan with boiling water halfway up the side of the terrine. Place the pan with the terrine in the middle of the oven and cook for approximately 1 1/4 hours. Test for doneness by inserting a skewer in the center of the terrine; it should be hot to the touch when removed.

Remove the terrine from the water bath and allow to cool on top of the stove for about 30 minutes. Peel back the aluminum foil from one end of the terrine and drain as much of the fat off as possible into a container that can be thrown away. Remove the aluminum foil and cover the terrine with a rectangle of waxed paper and one of fresh aluminum foil on top of it. Place a brick wrapped in aluminum foil (or another loaf pan filled with canned food or other weights) on top of the terrine and refrigerate for 24 to 48 hours — the longer, the better.

An hour or more before serving, remove the weights and place the terrine in a baking dish filled with warm water for a minute or two. Remove the aluminum foil and waxed paper and run a knife around the inside of the terrine to loosen from the pan. Cover the terrine with a cutting board and invert. Lift one end of the terrine and whack it down on the cutting board. Repeat with the other end if necessary. If the pâté does not come out immediately, tap the terrine all over with a knife handle and repeat the previous procedure if needed. Wrap the unmolded pâté in plastic wrap and refrigerate until ready to serve.

To serve the pâté, slice it thinly and arrange on small plates garnished with olives and cornichons. Serve with a sliced baguette and Dijon mustard or onion jam (page 33).

Pissaladière

When Bill and I first saw the Côte d'Azur in the 1970s, it still looked just as it does in Hitchcock's *To Catch a Thief*, and we fell hard for that incomparably beautiful landscape. To this day I get chills during the scene where Cary Grant serves lunch to a guest on his terrace overlooking a stunning view of Cap Ferrat. In the movie Grant serves quiche Lorraine, but the dish most people associate with that area is pissaladière.

In all of Provence, but especially Nice, pissaladière is available everywhere from street corners to elegant restaurants. The word derives from *pissalat*, meaning salted fish. It is similar to its Italian cousin, pizza, but never includes tomatoes or cheese.

We offered pissaladière at La Résidence as a first course. Served with a green salad, it also makes a satisfying lunch dish.

CRUST

1 1/2 c. all-purpose flour
1/2 t. salt
1/2 c. butter, cut into 1/2-inch pieces
2 T. olive oil
2–4 T. ice water

Mix flour and salt in food processor. Add cold butter and oil. Process, using on and off turns until mixture resembles coarse meal. Using on and off turns, mix in enough water, 1 T. at a time, to form moist clumps. Gather dough into ball, flatten, wrap in waxed paper, and chill for at least 2 hours.

FILLING

4 T. olive oil
8 c. sliced onions
3 cloves garlic, coarsely chopped
2 bay leaves
1 t. chopped fresh thyme
1 T. drained capers
salt and pepper to taste
20 or so black Mediterranean-style olives, such as Niçoises, pitted and cut in half
12–16 anchovy fillets

Heat oil in a heavy sauté pan. Add the onions, garlic, bay leaves, and thyme. Turn heat to medium low and cook for 20 minutes or more, stirring occasionally, until the onions are golden. Stir in the capers, discard the bay leaves, season with salt and pepper, and let cool to room temperature.

Preheat oven to 425°. Lightly oil a large baking sheet. Roll out the dough on a floured surface to an 11-inch circle. Transfer the dough to the prepared baking sheet. Crimp the edges of the dough to form a stand-up border.

Spread the onion filling evenly over the dough. Arrange olives and anchovies over the filling in a decorative pattern.

Bake 20 to 25 minutes or until the crust is golden.

Apple Celeriac Soup

Since Granny Smith apples are available all year, this soup is never out of season. In warm weather, we served it at the restaurant chilled, garnished with fresh mint. The winter version was heated, served with crème fraiche or sour cream and crumbled bacon on top.

Serves 4 to 6

3 T. butter
1 c. chopped leeks
1 c. chopped onion
2 c. peeled and chopped Granny Smith or Braeburn apples
1 medium celery root, peeled and chopped
(substitute 2 c. chopped celery if celery root is unavailable)
4 c. (or more) chicken stock
salt and pepper (preferably white) to taste
1/2 t. freshly grated nutmeg
1 1/2 t. grated orange zest
1/2–1 c. whipping cream or half-and-half
chopped fresh mint or crème fraiche and crumbled bacon

In a Dutch oven or large saucepan, sauté the vegetables and apples in butter over low heat until the leeks and onions are translucent. Add the stock. Bring to a boil, reduce heat, and simmer covered until the celery root is tender when pierced with a fork, about 20 minutes.

Purée the soup in a food processor or blender (in batches) until smooth. Pour the soup back into the saucepan, add salt, pepper, nutmeg, orange zest, and 1/2 c. cream. Add more chicken stock and/or cream if a thinner consistency is desired. Adjust seasonings.

Reheat to serve, or refrigerate until chilled and serve cold, with the garnish of choice.

Carrot Soup

Traditionally called *crème de Crécy*, this is one of the first soups we served at La Résidence. Tarragon and carrots are a traditional match in France, but not many Americans used tarragon in the 1970s; the flavor combination was new then and refreshingly different. This soup is appropriate any time of the year, served either warm or chilled.

The recipe can be easily adapted for spicier Asian-style soups by substituting Indian spices or fresh grated ginger (or both) for the tarragon.

Serves 4

3 T. butter
5 medium carrots, peeled and sliced
1 large boiling potato, peeled and sliced
3 leeks, white part only, washed well and chopped
4 c. chicken stock
2 t. dried tarragon
1 c. diced carrots
1/2 t. grated orange peel
1/8 t. grated fresh nutmeg
salt and pepper to taste
1/2 c. heavy cream or half-and-half
fresh chives and tarragon, chopped

Sauté the carrots, potatoes, and leeks in butter over medium heat until tender but not brown, about 5 minutes. Pour in 3 c. of the chicken stock, add the tarragon, and simmer the soup for 30 minutes. While the vegetables are cooking, simmer the diced carrots in the remaining c. of stock until barely tender, about 5 minutes, and reserve.

Purée the mixture in a food processor. If a thinner consistency is desired, add some of the reserved stock.

When ready to serve, stir in the heavy cream and orange peel. Reheat the soup, add the nutmeg, and serve garnished with the diced carrots and the chopped chives and tarragon.

Mushroom Soup Forestière

Serves 6

1/2 c. butter
2 c. chopped onions
3 lbs. mushrooms, sliced
1 c. Madeira
1 qt. rich chicken stock
2 bay leaves
1/2 c. heavy cream or half-and-half
salt and pepper to taste
chopped fresh chives

Sauté the onions in butter until soft and translucent. Add the mushrooms and continue cooking until they are tender. Pour in the stock and Madeira and add the bay leaves. Simmer for 30 minutes. Remove the bay leaves. In a food processor or with an immersion blender, pulse the soup for a few seconds. The consistency of the soup should be a little coarse.

To serve, add cream and reheat. Season with salt and pepper. Garnish with chopped chives.

Cream of Onion Soup

Serves 4 to 6

2 c. chopped onions
2 c. chopped leeks, white part only, washed well
1/2 c. Riesling
1/4 c. bourbon
3 c. chicken stock
2 t. fresh marjoram, chopped finely
1 bay leaf
1/2 c. heavy cream or half-and-half

a few dashes Tabasco sauce to taste
1/4 t. nutmeg
1 T. lemon zest
salt and pepper to taste

Sauté the onions and leeks in butter over medium-low heat until soft, without browning. Add Riesling, bourbon, stock, marjoram, and bay leaves. Simmer until the onions are quite mushy, about 30 minutes. Purée the soup in a food processor or blender in batches. Add cream. Reheat to serve. Add Tabasco, nutmeg, lemon zest, and salt and pepper just before serving.

Onion Soup Lyonnaise

This familiar style of onion soup is the perfect comfort food for a cold winter day. Its distinguishing ingredient is the duck stock, which we made from carcasses left over from all the various ways we served duck breast. Most of us don't have duck stock readily available, but a mixture of good chicken and beef stock makes an acceptable substitute.

Serves 6 to 8

3 large onions, peeled and chopped
1/2 c. clarified butter
1/4 c. brandy
6 c. duck stock (or a mixture of beef and chicken stock)
a few dashes Worcestershire sauce
salt and pepper to taste
homemade croutons (recipe follows)
2 c. grated Gruyère cheese

Sauté the onions in butter over low heat until they become soft and evenly golden. Add the brandy and ignite with a match. When the flame dies down, add the stock. Simmer 15 minutes. Season with Worcestershire, salt, and pepper.

Set the oven on broil. Ladle the soup into individual bowls or crocks. Float several croutons on top of the soup. Sprinkle a generous amount of cheese on top of the croutons. Place the bowls on a pan, and broil a few seconds until cheese is melted. Serve immediately.

LARGE CROUTONS

1 baguette (preferably a day or two old)
olive oil

Preheat oven to 450°. Cut a baguette into 1/2-inch slices and arrange on a large baking sheet. Drizzle generously with olive oil and bake until golden brown, turning once during cooking. Watch carefully to avoid burning.

Spring Soup

Shelling English peas was one of our rites of spring. We celebrated the season by adding this soup to the menu.

This recipe illustrates something that my father, Henry Hobbs, taught Bill. Almost any bland dish can be improved with the addition of lemon peel, Tabasco, and/or nutmeg—a combination that became known as "Neal spices" to Bill's protégés.

Serves 8 to 10

1 large onion, chopped
2 leeks, white part only, washed well and chopped
2 T. butter
4 c. chicken stock
10 oz. spinach, fresh or frozen
1 lb. shelled tiny English peas, fresh or frozen
1 bunch chopped watercress
1 1/2 c. half-and-half
salt and pepper to taste
1/4 t. nutmeg
1 t. grated lemon peel
3 dashes Tabasco sauce

In a Dutch oven, wilt the onions and leeks in butter just until they are tender and translucent. Cover with the stock and simmer 30 minutes.

Add the spinach, watercress, and peas (reserving a few of the peas for the garnish). Bring back to a simmer and immediately remove from heat. Purée in a blender or food processor. Pour the purée back into the Dutch oven and add the half-and-half. Season with salt and pepper, nutmeg, lemon peel, and Tabasco. Return to the stove and simmer for just a minute.

Serve hot or chilled, garnished with the reserved green peas.

Winter Soup

A lovely aromatic cold-weather bisque.

Serves 8 to 10

3 T. butter
1/2 butternut squash
1 small rutabaga
2 medium pears
2 medium apples
7 medium shallots
2 cloves garlic
5 c. or more chicken stock
1/2 c. white wine
1 stick cinnamon
1/8 t. ground cloves
2 bay leaves
2 T. sugar (optional)
1/2–1 c. heavy cream or half-and-half
salt and pepper to taste

Peel, seed, and roughly chop the fruits and vegetables. Sauté the shallots and garlic in the butter for a few minutes until tender. Add the remaining fruits and vegetables and continue to cook and stir over medium-low heat for about 5 minutes longer. Add chicken stock and white wine, cinnamon, cloves, bay leaves, and sugar. Simmer for 25 to 30 minutes or until the vegetables are very soft. Remove the cinnamon sticks and bay leaves.

Purée the mixture in a blender or food processor in batches. Before serving, reheat the soup, season with salt and pepper, and add 1/2 c. cream. If the soup is very thick, thin with more cream and stock. Adjust the seasonings.

CONDIMENTS

Onion Jam

When Bill made his country pâté at the restaurant, we always served it with onion jam. Unlike the time-consuming pâté, the jam is quite easy to make at home. It is a terrific complement to all kinds of meats, including roast beef and chicken. Try it with hamburgers and even ham biscuits, or on a cracker topped with a soft blue cheese.

Tightly covered, it will keep for several weeks in the refrigerator.

Makes 3 c.

2 large onions (about 4 c. sliced)
1/2 c. butter
1/2 c. sugar
3/4 c. red wine vinegar
2 t. black pepper
1 c. dry red wine
2 T. grenadine (optional)

Peel the onions, cut them in half lengthwise, and then cut each half into thin slices. In a large sauté pan, wilt the onions in butter until they are translucent, but not browned. Add the sugar, red wine vinegar, and black pepper. Cook very slowly until most of the liquid evaporates, about 20 minutes. Add the red wine and grenadine (the latter if a deeper red is desired). Simmer over low heat for another 30 minutes, stirring occasionally, until the mixture is thick and jammy.

This is better made a day or so before serving. Store it in the refrigerator to blend flavors. Bring to room temperature to serve.

Green Sauce

This brightly colored sauce was served at the restaurant on steak, usually a rib eye or New York strip. At home, use it to make boneless chicken breasts or even ground chuck a special treat.

Makes 3 c.

10 anchovy fillets
1 large clove garlic, minced
1/4 c. chopped cornichons (or dill pickles with seeds removed)
1/4 c. capers
1 c. extra virgin olive oil
1 T. Dijon mustard
3 T. mint leaves
1 c. parsley leaves
1 c. watercress, chopped coarsely
2 T. red wine vinegar
salt to taste

Place the anchovies, garlic, capers, cornichons, and a third of the olive oil in a food processor. Purée. Add the rest of the ingredients except the remaining oil and process. With the processor running, drizzle the remaining oil in slowly. Add salt to taste. Serve the sauce at room temperature over warm beef or chicken.

Ravigote Sauce

Recipes for ravigote vary almost as much as do those for its mayonnaise-based relatives rémoulade and tartar sauce. This was our version of ravigote sauce, a flavorful accompaniment to shrimp or fresh crabmeat.

Makes 2 c.

2 T. lemon juice
1 T. Dijon mustard
1 whole egg
1/4 t. salt
black pepper
1–1 1/2 c. olive oil
1 T. chopped chives
1 T. chopped tarragon
2 T. chopped parsley
2 T. finely chopped cornichons or gherkins
2 T. capers, chopped
4 anchovy fillets, chopped finely

Make a mayonnaise by placing the lemon juice, mustard, egg, salt, and pepper into a blender or food processor. Slowly drizzle in the oil until the sauce thickens, or emulsifies (for the technique, see the recipe for rosemary mayonnaise, page 13). Fold in the remaining herbs and anchovies and then chill. Serve with cold shrimp, crabmeat, or poached fish on a bed of lettuce garnished with hard-boiled eggs and tomato wedges.

Rouille

This sauce, originating from Marseille, is very similar to aioli. It is traditionally served with bouillabaisse, but it's also delicious with cold shrimp or other seafood.

Makes 1 1/2 c.

1/2 c. bread cubes (preferably a day or two old)
1 T. white wine vinegar
2 T. canned pimentos
3 cloves garlic, minced
2 egg yolks
1/4 t. salt

1/8 t. ground cayenne pepper
1/8 t. powdered saffron
3/4–1 c. extra virgin olive oil

Place all of the ingredients except the oil in a blender or food processor. Blend at medium speed a few seconds until the ingredients are well mixed. Leave the blender on while slowly drizzling the oil in a steady stream into the yolk mixture until the sauce thickens (emulsifies).

La Résidence House Vinaigrette

For the first year after opening the restaurant, we offered a small *salade verte* following the main course on our prix fixe menu. After the move to Chapel Hill and the switch to an à la carte menu, the salad became larger, the greens were more diverse, and the amount of mustard in the dressing was increased.

Here is the later version of our house vinaigrette, which is indeed quite heavy on the mustard. We changed the recipe after a visiting French chef shocked us by using almost as much mustard as vinegar in his salad dressing. We loved it.

This strong vinaigrette is particularly good with assertively flavored greens—watercress, curly endive, or arugula—in the salad mix. If the flavor is too bold or acidic for your taste, add an extra tablespoon or two of oil and a pinch of sugar.

Makes 1 1/4 c.

1/4 c. white wine vinegar
2 T. Dijon mustard (preferably Maille or Grey Poupon)
1 clove garlic, minced
1 t. finely minced shallot
salt and pepper to taste
3/4 c. olive oil (preferably Plagniol)

With a whisk blend together all of the ingredients except the oil. Gradually add the oil, whisking constantly. The dressing should be a thin emulsion.

Lemon Vinaigrette

Use this tangy dressing on mixed greens or other cold vegetables such as broccoli, asparagus, or green beans.

Makes 1 c.

1/4 c. lemon juice
1/4 t. grated lemon rind
1 t. Dijon mustard
1 t. finely chopped scallions
1 t. finely chopped parsley
1 T. tiny capers
pinch of sugar
salt and black pepper to taste
3/4 c. olive oil (preferably Plagniol)

Place all of the ingredients except the oil in a small jar or carafe. Cover and shake vigorously. Add the oil and shake again. Before serving, shake or stir to blend.

VEGETABLES AND SIDE DISHES

Asparagus with Brown Butter and Capers

This dish is a simple classic—both as an elegant appetizer by itself or as a side dish for grilled chicken or fish.

Serves 4

1 lb. cooked asparagus (see page 14)
1/2 c. butter
1/4 c. tiny capers
1 T. lemon juice

Melt the butter in a sauté pan and cook until it turns dark amber. Immediately add the asparagus and cook for a minute or two until just heated. Add lemon juice and capers, shaking the pan to distribute them evenly. With tongs, remove the asparagus onto the serving plate. Pour the sauce left in the pan over the vegetables and serve immediately.

Broccoli or Corn Timbales

Back in the 1970s we consumed eggs and cheese with abandon, blissfully unaware of the dangers of cholesterol. Timbales, or savory custards, though high in fat, can turn a tired vegetable into a special treat. La Résidence served timbales both as a first course and as a side dish.

Serves 6

6 eggs
2 c. finely chopped cooked broccoli or corn kernels
2 T. grated onion
1/2 c. bread crumbs
2 T. parsley, minced
1/2 c. Gruyère cheese, grated
3/4 c. half-and-half
salt and pepper to taste
a dash or two of Tabasco sauce
butter

Preheat oven to 325°.

Beat the eggs until well blended. Gently stir in all the remaining ingredients.

Heavily butter timbale molds or ramekins and ladle in the timbale mixture. Arrange the molds in a roasting pan. Pour in enough hot water to come halfway up the sides of the molds. Carefully slide into the oven and bake until the center is set—about 25 to 30 minutes. Remove the timbales from the pan and let cool for about 15 minutes. Then run a knife around the edge of the custard and unmold.

Serve with a little butter melted on top, or with a homemade tomato sauce (see page 20).

Grated Carrot Salad

A simple side dish encountered commonly in Southern France, this carrot dish was often part of the hors d'oeuvres variés platter at La Résidence. Later it migrated to Crook's Corner when Bill Smith became chef there in 1992. Smith likes to serve it next to an equally vivid red cabbage salad with fried soft-shelled crabs for a dramatically colorful presentation.

Serves 6

1 lb. peeled carrots (about 3 c.)
2 T. white wine vinegar
5 T. olive oil
2 cloves fresh garlic, minced
salt and pepper to taste
1 T. chopped fresh tarragon or 1 t. dried tarragon,
dried oregano or ground cumin (optional)
1 shallot, finely chopped (optional)

Grate the carrots in a food processor or hand grater. Whisk together the vinegar, oil, garlic, salt, and pepper. Add the grated carrots and, if desired, the optional ingredients. Mix well and let rest 30 minutes before serving.

La Res Potatoes

Our signature side dish, identified in French as *gratin dauphinois à la Résidence*, was served with most of the menu's meat dishes. This version omits the cheese usually seen in dauphinois; the large amount of garlic produces its rich flavor.

Our family makes this every Christmas to go with a rib roast—a sublime combination.

8 medium russet (baking) potatoes, about 3 1/2 lbs.
3 T. unsalted butter, melted
5 cloves garlic, minced
1 qt. half-and-half
1 c. heavy cream
salt and pepper to taste

Preheat oven to 350°.

Peel the potatoes and place them in a pot of cold water to keep them from turning brown.

Pour the melted butter into a 9 x 13-inch flame-proof baking pan or gratin dish. Sprinkle the garlic evenly around the bottom of the pan and rub into the melted butter.

Using a food processor or mandoline, slice the potatoes thinly (about 1/8-inch thick). Add the potatoes to the pan in layers, seasoning each layer generously with salt and pepper as you go. Add enough half-and-half to just cover the potatoes and place the pan over 2 stove-top burners on medium-high heat. When the half-and-half has just begun to bubble around the edges, pour the heavy cream over the top of the potatoes.

Bake the gratin for 40 to 50 minutes or until the potatoes are soft with a browned, crusty top. Allow the dish to sit for several minutes before serving.

Turned Potatoes

new (red or wax) potatoes, about 1 1/2 inches in diameter
butter
chopped fresh parsley

Cook the potatoes in boiling salted water for about 10 minutes or until they are tender when pierced with a fork. Remove from heat and immerse in ice water to stop cooking. With a paring knife, peel the skin from each potato around the circumference, leaving a cap of skin on the top and bottom. When ready to serve, heat the butter in a pan and add the potatoes. Cook just until warm. Serve sprinkled with parsley.

Ratatouille

This Provençal vegetable stew was served every day, sometimes as a warm side dish with lamb or roast chicken and sometimes as a cold appetizer, part of the hors d'oeuvres variés platter. Like most stews, ratatouille is just as good a day or so after being made if it is kept refrigerated.

Serves 8 to 10

1 large eggplant, peeled and cut into 1-inch cubes
2 medium onions
6 T. olive oil
2 red, green, or yellow bell peppers
2 zucchini, sliced into rounds or thick strips about 2 inches long
4 cloves garlic, minced
3 c. peeled, seeded, and chopped ripe or canned tomatoes
1 t. dried coriander
2 T. chopped fresh thyme (or 1 t. dried thyme)
salt and pepper to taste
4 T. chopped fresh basil (optional)

Place the eggplant in a colander and sprinkle lightly with salt. Let drain over the sink for an hour.

While the eggplant is draining, cut the onions in half lengthwise and then horizontally. Slice the onion pieces thinly and in a large sauté pan sauté in 2 T. of the oil over medium heat until translucent. Remove with a slotted spoon to a Dutch oven. Cut the peppers up in thick slices and sauté until just tender, adding a little more oil if necessary. Remove to the Dutch oven. Add more oil and sauté the zucchini until lightly browned on both sides. Drain the zucchini on paper towels and then add to the other cooked vegetables.

When the eggplant has finished draining, rub dry in paper towels and then sauté with the garlic in the remaining oil. Stir or shake the pan regularly to prevent sticking. Add the eggplant and garlic to the Dutch oven along with the tomatoes and herbs (except basil). Simmer over low heat, covered, for about 20 minutes, stirring occasionally to prevent sticking. (If the vegetables are sticking, add a little water, red wine, or tomato juice.) Season with salt and pepper.

Serve warm, cold, or at room temperature, garnished with fresh basil if you like.

Timbale of Spinach and Mint with Fresh Tomato Sauce

Bill chose this recipe to send to *Redbook* when the magazine requested a favorite dish for an article about promising young American chefs in 1981.

Serves 6

2 10-ounce packages fresh leaf spinach, washed, or 2 10-ounce packages frozen chopped spinach
1/2 c. fresh mint leaves
4 large eggs
1 1/2 c. half-and-half
1/2 c. finely grated Parmesan cheese
1 1/2 t. lemon juice
3 large cloves garlic, minced
3/4 t. salt
1/8 t. ground nutmeg
pinch of cayenne pepper
1/4 t. black pepper
1 T. olive oil
1/2 c. sliced scallions
3 c. peeled, seeded, and chopped tomatoes
peel of 1/2 large orange, removed with a vegetable peeler (not grated)
mint leaves and lemon slices

Preheat oven to 325°.

Cook fresh spinach in boiling water for 1 minute; drain. When cool enough to handle, squeeze with hands to remove as much water as possible. (If using frozen spinach, thaw and squeeze dry.) Put the spinach and mint in a food processor or blender. Process 10 to 15 seconds, until finely chopped.

Beat the eggs in a large bowl. Add the spinach mixture, half-and-half, cheese, lemon juice, 1/4 t. of the garlic, 1/2 t. of the salt, the nutmeg, cayenne, and 1/4 t. black pepper; mix well. Pour into a buttered 8-inch-long loaf pan. Bake 50 to 55 minutes, until center is just set.

Meanwhile, in a large skillet, heat oil over moderately high heat. Add scallions and cook 1 minute, stirring frequently, until soft but not brown. Add the tomatoes, the orange peel, the remaining garlic, 1/4 t. salt, and a few grains of pepper. Simmer 20 minutes, stirring frequently, until most of the liquid has evaporated and the sauce is thick. Discard the orange peel.

Remove the timbale from the oven and let stand 5 minutes. Turn out onto a serving plate; garnish with mint and lemon. Slice and serve with the tomato sauce.

White Bean Casserole

This pairs beautifully with most any kind of lamb dish.

Serves 10 to 12

1 lb. dry great northern white beans
1 small onion
3 whole cloves
3 bay leaves
1 t. salt and freshly ground black pepper to taste
3 cloves garlic, cut in half
2 slices of uncooked bacon, cut into pieces
4 T. olive oil
2 small zucchini
1 medium onion
3 cloves garlic, minced
1 28-oz. can whole tomatoes
salt and pepper to taste
chopped parsley

Soak the beans overnight.

Pick over beans and remove pebbles, skins, and other detritus. Place the beans in a large pot and cover with water so that there is an inch of water above the beans. Peel the small onion, and, using a small knife, make 3 cross incisions around side of the onion and insert 1 whole clove in each incision. Add a small onion, bay leaves, salt and pepper, 3 halved cloves of garlic, and bacon to the beans and bring to a boil. Reduce heat and simmer, covered, about 30 minutes or until just done.

Preheat oven to 350°.

Scrub the zucchini and cut into 1/4-inch rounds. Heat 2 T. of olive oil over high heat, add the zucchini in a single layer and season with salt and pepper. Sauté until lightly browned on both sides. Drain on paper towels.

Peel a medium onion, slice in half lengthwise, then cut each half cross-wise. Slice each quarter to make 1/4-inch strips. Sauté in 2 T. of oil over medium-high heat until translucent. Add 3 cloves of minced garlic and sauté 2 minutes more. Remove to paper towels and reserve.

Drain the tomatoes; seed and chop them coarsely. Combine the beans, zucchini, onions, garlic, and tomatoes in an ovenproof casserole; cover and cook for 45 minutes. Adjust seasoning. Sprinkle with chopped parsley and serve. This dish can be made in advance.

White Bean Purée

This lovely simple side dish, common in the winter months throughout Southern France, is true comfort food. At La Résidence we served it with grilled leg of lamb during the early years before outdoor grilling at Chapel Hill restaurants was prohibited. It is also compatible with most any kind of game, especially duck.

Serves 8 to 10

1 lb. white beans (great northern, navy, or cannellini)
5 large cloves garlic, peeled
1 1/2 T. fresh tarragon, minced
2 t. salt

1/4 c. olive oil
6 c. water

Soak the beans in water overnight. Drain and put the beans into a large Dutch oven along with the rest of the ingredients. Simmer for 1 1/2 hours or until the beans are quite soft. If too much water evaporates, add a little more. Drain the beans, reserving the liquid.

Purée the beans in 2 batches in a processor, adding 1/4 c. of liquid for each batch. Taste and add more salt if necessary.

Zucchini Delight

Bill and I usually spent Christmas holidays visiting my large family in Mississippi. My grandmother's traditional Christmas feast included roast beef, buttered new potatoes, and a green bean casserole topped, 1950s-style, with canned crumbled onion rings. Gradually Bill, always game to cook even on vacation, took over the holiday menu, first adding "La Res Potatoes," which were a big success. The next year he replaced the traditional green beans with this side dish we favored at La Résidence, which we jokingly referred to as "zucchini delight." To this day my siblings replicate this menu every Christmas.

Delightfully easy to make, zucchini delight is even better in the summer season made from squash picked fresh from the garden.

Serves 4 to 6

4 medium zucchini
2 cloves garlic, minced
4 T. butter
salt and pepper to taste

At least an hour before serving, coarsely grate the zucchini. Sprinkle with a little salt and drain in a colander until ready to cook. Melt the butter in a sauté pan. Add the garlic and cook for 1 minute over low heat. Add the grated zucchini, and cook until tender—just a few minutes. Season with salt and pepper and serve immediately.

Bouillabaisse

During a trip to France in 1976, Bill and I visited a friend's parents in Arles. There we discovered one of Provence's many similarities to the American South—French Southerners are as warm and hospitable as their counterparts in America. Our hosts, the Bertaudons, treated us like family, insisting on celebrating our visit by making their own traditional bouillabaisse, a production involving a day's preparation.

Bill tried to re-create that sublime bouillabaisse at our restaurant. He substituted Atlantic fish for Mediterranean and came up with this North Carolina version of the Marseilles specialty. Bill Smith carried on the tradition until 1992. Even now when he entertains veteran staff members, they invariably request this bouillabaisse with all the fixings.

Serves 10 to 12

4 T. olive oil
2 large onions, coarsely chopped
3 leeks, well cleaned and coarsely chopped
4 cloves garlic, chopped
4 carrots, peeled and cut into large slices
1 28-oz. can diced tomatoes, including liquid
2 qts. rich fish stock or clam juice
zest of 1 orange (peeled with a vegetable peeler, not grated)
2 bay leaves
1/2 t. crushed fennel seeds
1/2 t. saffron
1 t. dried thyme
1 T. crushed red pepper
2 c. dry vermouth
1/4 c. Pernod
4 lbs. fresh Atlantic seafood: mussels, shrimp, scallops, and firm-fleshed white fish—
such as monkfish, trigger fish, grouper, or cod—cut into small pieces
turned potatoes (page 40, omitting butter and parsley)

chopped parsley
homemade croutons (page 31)
rouille (page 35)

In a large Dutch oven, heat the olive oil. Sauté the onions, leeks, garlic, and carrots in the olive oil until just soft. Add the rest of the ingredients except the seafood. Simmer for 1 hour. Reserve until ready to serve.

Just before serving, reheat the soup to the boiling point. Add seafood and the turned potatoes. Simmer for a few minutes until seafood is cooked.

Serve topped with a crouton and parsley and a small crock of rouille on the side.

Paella

Unlike the eastern side of Provence, which adjoins Liguria, the Rhône River port of Arles is decidedly Spanish-oriented, in part because of the multitude of Basque and other Iberian refugees who flocked to the city after the Spanish Civil War.

As Bill and I strolled around this old city, our friend Jean-Claude pointed out the famous bullfighter hangout Place du Forum. The outdoor cafés surrounding the square specialize in paella, more commonly associated with the northern Spanish coast. Paella Camarguaise is distinctive for its use of rice grown in the Camargue, the Rhône delta just south of Arles.

We tried to re-create that Arles-style paella once we got back to the restaurant. If you can find the fragrant Camargue rice, by all means try it with this recipe. We substituted American long-grain rice.

Serves 6 to 8

4 T. olive oil
1 chicken, cut into 8 pieces, or 8 thighs and legs
1 lb. chorizo sausage, cut into 1/2-inch slices
1 large onion, roughly chopped
1 c. chopped bell peppers (any color, preferably a mixture of red and green)
3 cloves garlic, minced
1 14-oz. can diced tomatoes

1/2 t. saffron
1 t. paprika
1/2 t. ground coriander
1 t. minced fresh thyme leaves
salt and pepper
1 c. vermouth or other dry white wine
4 c. or more chicken broth
2 c. short- or medium-grain rice
16 or more large shrimp, peeled
16 or more clams in the shell
1 c. squid, cut into rings (optional)
2 c. tiny green peas
3 T. capers
1/2 c. Mediterranean-style pitted olives, black or green
parsley
lemon wedges

In a paella pan, deep sauté pan, or Dutch oven, brown the chicken in half of the olive oil. Remove to a plate and sauté the chorizo for several minutes. Reserve. Sauté the onions, peppers, and garlic in the rest of the oil just until tender. Add the tomatoes, seasonings, vermouth, and 4 c. of the broth.

Bring the liquid to a simmer. Add the rice, push under the liquid, and simmer without stirring for 10 minutes. Add the shrimp, clams, squid, and peas, pushing the ingredients down under the unabsorbed liquid.

Cover the pan and simmer for another 5 minutes or until the rice is tender. The paella should be a bit juicy—if the rice seems too dry, add a small amount of warm broth.

Remove from heat and sprinkle with capers and olives. Cover and let sit for a few minutes before serving garnished with parsley and lemon wedges.

Mountain Trout à la Bonne Femme

In 1975 Bill and I visited the mountains near Highlands, North Carolina, to dine at a tiny restaurant with a stellar reputation. The owners of the remote Frog and Owl were Mark Rosenstein, now owner and chef of the superb

Marketplace in Asheville, North Carolina, and his wife Jerry. Mark served rainbow trout fresh from the stream outside the restaurant, a renovated old mill. Smitten with the delicate flavor of that lovely fish, we found a supplier who would drive all the way to Chatham County on Thursdays. From then on, we served mountain trout every weekend.

A la bonne femme refers to the classic Burgundian combination of potatoes and onions. In France these ingredients often accompany sole or chicken, but we liked them with North Carolina mountain trout even better. This dish can also be made with fresh flounder.

For 1 serving

1 medium russet potato, peeled
1 cleaned whole mountain (rainbow) trout or 1 large trout fillet
flour
salt
2 T. clarified butter
2 pieces bacon, chopped
1/4 c. chopped scallions
1/4 c. chopped celery
1 T. chopped celery leaves
1 T. chopped parsley
salt and pepper to taste
1 t. lemon juice
lemon wedge

Preheat oven to 200°.

Cut off the ends and sides of the potato to make a rectangular shape. Dice into 1/2-inch cubes and blanch in boiling water for 4 minutes. Drain and rinse with cold water.

Mix the flour and salt. Heat the butter in a sauté pan over medium-high heat. Dredge the trout in the flour. Sauté the fish a few minutes on each side until golden brown. Remove the fish from the pan and keep in a warm oven.

To the same pan add the raw bacon; brown for a minute, and add the potatoes. Sauté over medium-high heat for 5 to 6 minutes until the bacon is thoroughly cooked and the potatoes become golden. Remove with a slotted spoon and drain on paper towels. Add the chopped scallions, celery, and herbs to the pan and cook for another few minutes until the celery is soft. Return the potatoes and bacon to the pan. Mix all of the ingredients and season with salt and pepper. Add a squeeze of lemon juice and pour over the trout to serve. Garnish with a lemon wedge.

Trout Provençale

Trout is not a fish associated with Provence, but the traditional Provençal flavors of this sauce beautifully enhance North Carolina mountain trout or any mild white-fleshed fish.

Serves 2

2 cleaned whole mountain trout
2 cloves garlic, peeled and pressed lightly with the side of a knife
flour
salt and pepper
4 T. butter, preferably clarified
1 T. olive oil
1 c. finely julienned fennel bulb
1 c. sliced mushrooms
1 ripe tomato, peeled, seeded, and chopped coarsely
juice of 1 orange
1 T. grated orange zest
2 T. Pernod (optional)
2 T. butter cut in small pieces
salt and pepper to taste

Preheat oven to 200°.

Rub the inside of the trout with garlic. Mix flour with salt and pepper. Dredge the trout in the flour, covering both sides. Sauté the fish in 2 T. of the butter and the olive oil over medium heat until golden and cooked through, about 4 minutes on each side. Place the trout on a warm plate and set in a warm oven while making the vegetables and sauce.

Finely chop the garlic you used to rub the fish. Wipe the sauté pan clean.

In the remaining 2 T. of butter, sauté the fennel for several minutes. Add the mushrooms and continuing sautéing for several minutes more until the vegetables are just tender. Add the tomatoes, half of the orange juice, the orange zest, and the Pernod and sauté for another minute. Remove the vegetables with a slotted spoon, leaving the liquids in the pan. Place the vegetables on top of the trout. Add the rest of the orange juice to the pan and reduce over medium heat just a few minutes until the sauce thickens slightly. Whisk in the butter quickly, season with salt and pepper; then spoon the sauce over the fish and serve.

Trout Rolls with Ginger-Mushroom Filling

In 1978 Bill teamed up with Chinese cookbook writer Olivia Wu for a series of cooking classes held in La Résidence's new digs in town. Their "East meets West" collaboration resulted in several interesting hybrid dishes and initiated a new creative era for Bill. This departure from more classical French dishes broadened the scope of the menu and foreshadowed the controversial "fusion" or "global" trend that has permeated restaurant menus for the past decade. Olivia was the inspiration for this recipe, which Bill created for *Bon Appétit* magazine.

Serves 4

4 trout fillets, skinned
1 T. cornstarch
6 1/2 T. peanut oil
1 1/2 T. minced fresh ginger root
2 cloves garlic, minced
5 medium mushrooms, minced (3/4 c.)
3 scallions, minced (1/2 c.)
1 T. dry sherry or Chinese rice wine
5 T. soy sauce
1 package (8 oz.) cellophane noodles (also called bean thread or transparent noodles)

1 T. oriental sesame oil
a few dashes Tabasco sauce or chili oil
2 scallions, thinly sliced
5 fresh asparagus spears, cut on the diagonal into 1/2-inch slices
finely chopped cilantro (optional)

Cut each fillet in half crosswise. Place each piece between 2 sheets of waxed paper, sprinkling the fillets first with a little cornstarch to prevent sticking. Using a meat pounder or the flat side of a cleaver, gently pound the fillets until they are about 1/8-inch thick. Check to make sure they are not sticking; add additional cornstarch if necessary. Refrigerate until needed.

In a medium skillet or wok, heat 2 1/2 T. of the oil over high heat. Add the ginger root and stir for about 1 minute. Add the garlic, mushrooms, and scallions and cook for 2 to 3 minutes, or until the liquid from the mushrooms is absorbed. Off the heat, stir in the sherry or rice wine and 1 T. of the soy sauce; let cool to room temperature.

Place the noodles in a large bowl and pour 4 c. of boiling water over them. Leave for about 5 minutes, or until tender. Drain and place in a bowl of ice-cold water for about 10 minutes (this keeps them from sticking together). Drain the noodles and separate the strands with your hands. Place in a large bowl and add 3 T. soy sauce, sesame oil, and hot sauce to taste. Add the sliced scallions and toss. Reserve.

Place about 1 heaping T. of the ginger-mushroom filling along the long side of a pounded fillet. Starting at the filled side, roll tightly into a cigarette shape. (If the fillet doesn't stick together, use equal amounts of cornstarch and water to make a paste; dab a little along the edges to help the ends stick together.) Repeat with the additional fillets.

In a medium skillet, heat 1 T. of oil over high heat. When the oil is sizzling, add the asparagus and stir-fry for about 30 seconds, or until slightly cooked, but still crunchy.

In a large skillet, heat the remaining 3 T. oil over medium-high heat until hot. Add the fillets, seam-side down, and sauté for 2 to 3 minutes on each side, turning gently, until cooked through. Add 1 T. of the soy sauce during the last minute of cooking.

Place the seasoned noodles on a serving plate and the trout rolls on top.

Scatter the sautéed asparagus around the sides of the fish and sprinkle with the chopped cilantro.

Serve warm or cold.

Filet Mignon with Composed Butter

No matter how many different ways La Res served beef, filet mignon was the most popular choice. Served with one of our composed butters, this tender cut complements a fine Bordeaux or California Cabernet beautifully.

These simple composed butters can be made ahead and keep well in the refrigerator for a couple of days or in the freezer for weeks, if wrapped tightly. They need not accompany an expensive cut of meat and do wonders for other cuts of beef, chicken, in some cases fish, and even baked potatoes.

Serves 2

composed butter (recipes follow)
2 1 1/4-inch-thick filets mignons

The same method is used in making all of the composed butters listed below: Let the butter soften to room temperature. Beat the butter lightly with a whisk or an electric beater. Stir in the other ingredients. Shape into a log about 3 inches in diameter, then wrap with waxed paper or Saran wrap and chill for at least an hour. When ready to cook the steaks, cut the butter into 1/2-inch slices.

To cook the steaks, simply heat a small amount of vegetable oil in a heavy frying pan to medium high. At the same time turn your oven broiler to high.

Fry the steaks in the hot pan for 3 to 4 minutes on each side (for rare). Remove and place on a broiler pan. Place the composed butter slice on top. Broil for a few seconds until slightly melted before serving.

Garnish with finely chopped parsley.

GREEN PEPPERCORN BUTTER

1 stick (1/2 c.) unsalted butter
1 T. green peppercorns

1 T. finely minced shallot
2 t. lemon juice
salt to taste

MUSHROOM BUTTER

1 stick (1/2 c.) unsalted butter
1 c. finely chopped mushrooms (mixed varieties)
1/4 c. soy sauce
1 T. minced shallot
1 small head roasted garlic, peeled and minced
1 t. lemon juice
salt to taste

MUSTARD BUTTER

1 stick (1/2 c.) unsalted butter
1 T. Dijon mustard
4 t. grainy mustard (such as Pommery)
1 small clove garlic, minced
1 T. minced shallot
1 t. lemon juice
salt to taste

NIÇOISE OLIVE BUTTER

1 stick (1/2 c.) unsalted butter
1 clove garlic, minced
2 oil-packed sun-dried tomatoes, chopped finely
1 anchovy, minced finely
1 T. finely chopped parsley
1 t. lemon juice
1 t. grated lemon rind
1/4 c. finely chopped Niçoise or other black olives
salt to taste (take care—the olives and anchovy are salty)

1 stick (1/2 c.) unsalted butter
1 T. each: minced shallots, parsley, chives, and red onion
1 t. lemon juice
salt and pepper to taste
1/4 c. Roquefort or other good-quality blue cheese such as Stilton or Gorgonzola
1/2 c. chopped toasted walnuts
salt to taste

For Roquefort Walnut Butter, mix all of the ingredients according to the master recipe except the walnuts. Sprinkle the nuts on top of the butter after broiling.

Boeuf en Daube Provençale

La Résidence opened on May 8, 1976, in the old Fearrington family homestead 8 miles south of Chapel Hill. The menu read:

Pâté de campagne
Daube provençale
ou
Filet de poisson Alphonse
Salade verte
Gâteau au citron

The price was $10.00. Forbidden by Chatham County law to sell alcohol of any kind, we had to tell guests who wanted wine with their meal to brown-bag their own. We charged a corkage fee of $2.00.

I've long since forgotten who or what "Alphonse" was or what kind of fish we used, but *boeuf en daube* is a traditional Southern French beef stew with wine and olives. *Daube* refers to the earthenware dish in which it is cooked and served in that part of the world. As the menu grew, customer demand for this peasant-style stew waned in favor of filet mignon with a variety of sauces and butters, but we served it for staff supper for years. It's a good company dish to cook ahead of time. The flavors meld and improve with time, up to a day or two after the dish is made.

Serves 6 to 8

5 T. olive oil or bacon fat
4 large carrots, peeled and cut in slices
1 large or 2 medium onions, peeled and sliced thickly
3 1/2 pounds beef chuck or round, cut into 1 1/2-inch cubes
1 bottle red wine, preferably Côte du Rhône or a Syrah/Grenache blend
2 T. tomato paste
3 c. beef broth
3 bay leaves
1 T. dried thyme
1/4 t. ground cloves
2 t. grated orange peel
1 t. salt
2 t. freshly ground black pepper
3/4 c. Mediterranean-style black olives, pitted
1 lb. cooked wide flat noodles
2–3 T. chopped parsley

Heat 3 T. of the oil or fat in a Dutch oven. Add the carrots and onions and sauté over medium-high heat until the onions are translucent, about 5 minutes. Remove the vegetables.

Pour the remaining 2 T. oil or fat in a sauté pan over medium-high heat. Add the beef and brown on all sides. Pour the beef and pan juices into the Dutch oven with the vegetables.

Add the wine, tomato paste, broth, and seasonings. Cover and bring to a boil. Reduce to very low heat and simmer slowly, stirring occasionally, for 2 1/2 to 3 hours, or until the meat is tender.

Remove the beef to a bowl with a slotted spoon. In a blender or food processor, purée the vegetable and broth mixture and then return the mixture to the Dutch oven along with the beef. (If you have an immersion blender, you can purée the vegetables in the pot.) Add olives and correct seasonings.

Serve over noodles garnished with parsley.

LA RÉSIDENCE

Calf's Liver with Avocado

Calf's liver is an acquired taste for most people. Look for the pinkest liver you can find, which has a more delicate flavor. This simple but elegant preparation may not convert you; but if you are a liver lover, this dish is an interesting departure from the more predictable pairing of liver and onions.

Serves 4

1 calf's liver, very thinly sliced
1 c. fine bread crumbs
3 T. clarified butter
2 firm avocados, sliced
6 scallions, chopped
8 lemon wedges

Dry the liver with paper towels. Dredge the slices in bread crumbs to coat. In a sauté pan, cook the liver slices in the butter over high heat until brown, about 1 minute on each side. Place on a warm plate.

In the same pan, sauté the avocado slices briefly, just until warm. Add scallions and sauté for another minute or two.

Arrange the avocados in a fan shape on top of the liver. Sprinkle the scallions on top. Garnish each plate with 2 lemon wedges before serving.

Chicken Stuffed with Spinach and Cheese

This recipe was adapted by Judith Olney from her brother-in-law Richard Olney's *Simple French Cooking*. It was a big hit with Bill and the other members of Judith's 1973 cooking class. These women, all knowledgeable cooks, began to gather every month or so with Bill, and later with me, to experiment with new recipes. They urged Bill and me to leave the Villa Teo and go out on our own. When we did, they became our most devoted patrons. Over the years, they helped us develop many new recipes for the menu.

This convivial group still meets regularly to cook and, of course, to eat. Just recently we revisited this old favorite, adding a splash of scuppernong wine to the pan juices, as Bill sometimes did. We all agreed it was as delicious as we remembered but thought it should be renamed "chicken with green pantaloons."

Serves 4

1 small fresh chicken, split on the bottom with backbone removed
3 T. olive oil
1 t. mixed dried herbs (e.g., thyme, savory, oregano)
1 medium onion, chopped finely
5 T. butter at room temperature
8 oz. chopped spinach
4 T. chopped mushrooms (optional)
1 t. fresh marjoram
3 oz. cream cheese
1 egg, lightly beaten
1/4 c. Parmesan cheese
salt and pepper to taste

An hour or so before cooking, rub the chicken with olive oil, salt and pepper, and dried herbs and set aside while you make the stuffing.

Preheat oven to 450°.

Sauté the onion in 3 T. butter. When the onion softens add the spinach and mushrooms. Cook until the vegetables are tender, just a few minutes. Squeeze out excess water from the spinach.

Mix together the remaining softened butter, marjoram, cream cheese, egg, and Parmesan. Season with salt and pepper. Stir in the spinach mixture.

Lift the skin up carefully from the breast, legs, and thighs. Slide the filling under the skin, pushing until it forms a thick layer around the flesh of the chicken.

Roast for 10 minutes. Turn heat down to 375°, and continue to cook, basting every 20 minutes, until done, about 50 minutes more. If the chicken seems to be browning too fast, cover with foil for the remainder of the cooking time.

Bill Neal and Jane Helsel in the kitchen at La Résidence in Fearrington Village, 1977.

Moreton Neal, Bill Smith, and the kitchen staff at La Résidence in Chapel Hill, 1982.

Chicken with 40 Cloves of Garlic

This homey Southern French classic was never quite fancy enough to become a popular menu item, but it was always a big hit at staff supper.

Serves 4

3–4 heads garlic, divided into cloves, unpeeled (approximately forty cloves)
1 medium-sized chicken, cut into pieces
2 T. olive oil
1 1/2 c. chicken broth
1/2 c. dry Chardonnay
1 t. herbes de Provence
salt and black pepper to taste

Sauté chicken pieces in oil over a medium-hot flame until golden. Add garlic and sauté for 2 minutes. Add liquids and herbs. Simmer until chicken is cooked and sauce is reduced, about 30 minutes. Serve with boiled new potatoes.

Duck with Red Wine and Shallots

Serves 6 to 8

3 4 1/2- to 5-lb. ducklings
3 large carrots, chopped
3 large celery stalks, chopped
1 large onion, chopped
1 1/2 T. salt mixed with 20–25 turns of freshly ground pepper
9 cloves garlic, crushed
1 medium onion, quartered
1 bottle red wine
3 T. clarified butter
3 T. flour
1/2 c. chopped celery

1/2 c. chopped onion
1/2 c. chopped carrots
4 T. butter, cut into small pieces
salt and pepper to taste
6 shallots, finely chopped
chopped parsley

Preheat oven to 450°.

Remove the necks and giblets from the duck cavities. Discard the livers or reserve for another use. Wash the ducks thoroughly inside and out. Pat dry with paper towels. Cut off the duck tails, the wings below first joint, and the neck skin flaps. Scatter necks, tails, wings, and giblets on a large baking sheet, along with chopped carrots, celery stalks, and onion. Place in a 450° oven for approximately 40 minutes until well browned, turning the duck parts once during cooking.

Season the inside of the ducks generously with salt and pepper. Place an onion quarter and 3 crushed garlic cloves in each duck cavity. Truss the ducks by making a 1- to 2-inch incision about 2 inches from the tail end and cavity opening. Work leg bone through incision.

Remove the baking sheet from the oven and carefully pour off the fat. Deglaze the baking sheet with some of the red wine and scrape duck parts, vegetables, and pan scrapings into a stock pot. Add red wine, leaving half the bottle in reserve. Add 12 c. water and bring to a boil over high heat. Reduce heat to medium high and continue cooking uncovered for about an hour, until reduced by two-thirds. Strain through a colander and then a fine-mesh strainer. You should have approximately 4 c. of liquid.

To make a brown sauce, heat the clarified butter in a heavy-bottomed pot over medium high, add the flour, and cook, whisking constantly until the mixture (roux) is a nutty brown. Add chopped celery, onion, and carrots and stir to combine with the roux; cook over medium low heat another 5 minutes. Add the stock and the remaining half-bottle of wine. Bring to a boil and reduce to a simmer. Simmer, partially covered, over low heat approximately 45 minutes. While the sauce is cooking, skim off the grease occasionally with a large spoon. Strain the sauce into a saucepan through a fine-mesh strainer, pressing all the liquid out of the vegetables, with the back of a spoon. Bring the sauce back to a gentle boil; skim any remaining grease from surface. Remove from heat.

While the sauce is cooking, place ducks on a wire rack in a roasting pan, breast-side up, and put on a rack in the bottom third of the oven. After 10 minutes, reduce heat to 400°. Roast another 30 minutes. Remove ducks from oven and cool.

Cut the leg section off the ducks. Then make an incision down the center of the breast bone, and bone the breast meat off each side of the carcass, leaving it intact with the wing. (The carcasses can be used for making stock.) The duck should be medium rare at this point. If you prefer the breast meat that way, reserve it and just before serving remove the skin and slice the breast pieces. Otherwise, place the breasts together with the legs in a roasting pan and roast for another 20 minutes at 400° until the skin is crispy.

Just before serving, bring the sauce to a boil and turn off heat. Whisk butter in bit by bit, working quickly so that the butter is incorporated into the sauce before it melts. Stir in salt and pepper. Ladle some sauce onto a warm plate. Place the duck on top of the sauce and sprinkle with shallots and parsley.

Duck Breasts with Sauce Carroll

Sauce Carroll was named for our dear friend the late Carroll Kyser. When we first opened La Résidence in the country, Carroll rented part of the farmhouse for use as a cooking school. Her mother, Georgia, helped us decorate the original restaurant, and her husband Jay Bryan was one of our first waiters.

Whether she taught us this recipe or simply loved to eat it, I don't recall. What lingers in my memory is the enjoyment of many happy "tastings" with Bill, Carroll, Jay, and Georgia as we developed recipes for the restaurant menu.

It is not easy to find boneless duck breasts, so you will probably have to buy whole ducks and bone them. The legs can be reserved for other uses, such as confit or cassoulet, and the carcasses can be used to make stock.

Serves 6 to 8

3 lemons
1/3 c. sugar
3 T. red wine vinegar
1/3 c. cognac
2 c. brown sauce made from 4 c. duck stock or
2 c. each of beef stock and chicken stock
1 T. olive oil
6 boneless duck breast halves
salt and pepper
4 T. butter
1 bunch watercress

Using a vegetable peeler, carefully remove the lemon peel in long strips. Slice the pieces into very thin strips (julienne). Blanch in boiling water for several minutes. Drain and reserve. Juice the lemons and reserve.

In a large saucepan, bring the sugar and vinegar to a boil, without stirring, and continue cooking until the sugar caramelizes. Stir in the blanched lemon peel, then add the cognac and ignite. Add the brown sauce and simmer for 30 minutes, skimming off any fat from the surface. Reserve until ready to serve.

Heat the oil in a heavy, large skillet over medium-high heat. Season the duck breasts with salt and pepper; add to the skillet skin-side down and cook 5 to 8 minutes. Turn and cook about 2 minutes longer for medium rare. Transfer to heated plate and cover loosely with foil to keep warm.

Bring the sauce to a boil and remove from heat. Add lemon juice 1 T. at time until the sauce achieves a slight tartness. Whisk the butter in bit by bit, working quickly so that the butter is incorporated into the sauce before it melts. Season with salt and pepper.

Thinly slice the duck breasts on the diagonal and arrange on each plate. Liberally spoon sauce on top. Garnish with a few sprigs of watercress before serving.

Cassoulet

Duck breast was a popular menu choice at the restaurant. This left the thighs and legs of the birds to be preserved in spices and duck fat, a method that produces the delicious confit. Cassoulet, a southwestern French casserole, is the perfect vehicle for duck confit. After we moved to Chapel Hill, we served this in cold weather as an early supper special.

If like most of us, you don't have the time or equipment for homemade duck confit, simply season the duck legs with salt and pepper and roast them for 30 minutes in a 450° oven. Even with roast duck, or no duck at all, this cassoulet makes a terrific winter supper dish. The leftovers are even better the next day.

Serves 10 to 12

2 c. dried white beans
3 T. olive oil
8 small or 4 large lamb shanks
8 duck legs, confit or roasted (optional)
3 carrots, diced
1 large onion, diced
2 celery stalks with leaves, diced
5 cloves garlic, minced
1 1/2 c. white wine
2–3 c. lamb or chicken stock
1 14-oz. can diced tomatoes
1/4 c. tomato paste, or 1/2 c. tomato sauce
2 t. grated lemon zest
2 t. fresh or 1 t. dried thyme
2 bay leaves
1 lb. kielbasa or French garlic sausage, cut into slices
salt and pepper to taste
bread crumbs

Soak the beans overnight in water. Drain.

In a large Dutch oven or stock pot, brown the lamb shanks in olive oil in

2 batches. Reserve. Add more oil or bacon fat if necessary, and sauté the diced onions, carrots, and celery over medium heat until soft, approximately 10 minutes. Add garlic and sauté 2 more minutes. Add the lamb shanks, wine, stock, tomatoes, tomato paste or sauce, zest, herbs, beans, sausage, and duck legs if you like.

Simmer over very low heat, covered, for 3 1/2 to 4 hours, stirring occasionally, until beans are soft and shanks are falling off the bone. Add more stock if necessary to keep the stew moist.

When the cassoulet is done, remove the meat from its bones. Tear meat into large chunks and stir back into the beans. Let rest for at least an hour before serving. Just before serving, sprinkle the top with bread crumbs. Reheat in a 350° oven until the bread crumbs are golden and cassoulet is hot.

Lamb Curry

On our first trip to Paris in 1977, Bill and I headed for the legendary Left Bank bistro La Coupole, known more for its famous literary clientele than for its food. We were pleasantly surprised by the bistro's exceptional lamb curry. It made such an impression that Bill tried to replicate the recipe at home and later served it at La Res on the early supper menu.

Serves 6

4 T. olive oil
2 1/2 lbs. lamb shoulder, cubed
2 c. chopped onion
3 cloves garlic, minced (about 2 T.)
2 t. minced fresh ginger
2 T. mild or hot curry powder
1/2 t. ground coriander
1 t. cumin
salt and pepper to taste
4 T. flour
1 14-oz. can diced tomatoes, including liquid
1 1/2 c. beef stock

1/2 c. raisins, preferably golden
1 t. lemon zest
1 T. lemon juice
1 large Granny Smith apple, peeled and cut into cubes
fresh cilantro
mint chutney

Brown the lamb, in batches, in half the oil. Set lamb aside on a plate and sauté the onion in the remaining oil until soft. Add the garlic and ginger, and sauté 1 minute. Add the dry seasonings and flour; continue cooking while stirring, 2 minutes longer. Add the tomatoes with their liquid, stock, raisins, lemon zest, and lemon juice. Simmer 1 1/4 hour, stirring occasionally. Add the apple cubes and continue to cook 1/2 hour longer.

Garnish with fresh chopped cilantro and serve over rice or couscous. Mint chutney can be found at Asian grocery stores and is the perfect accompaniment for this dish. If the chutney is unavailable, substitute fresh mint for the cilantro.

Grilled Leg of Lamb

One of our stops on a trip to the Côte d'Azur in the mid-1970s was La Colombe d'Or in Saint Paul de Vence. This lovely inn, a haunt of Picasso, Léger, Matisse, and other artists who traded paintings for meals, is now known more for its art collection than its food, but its restaurant is still a bastion of traditional Provençal specialties. The grilled lamb we tasted there served with white bean purée was a sensation.

Bill tried to re-create it on a flimsy grill parked outside the kitchen door. He used applewood branches from the Fearrington's orchard, which added a lovely flavor. Friends and customers loved it, but the dish did not survive the move to Chapel Hill, where town restrictions prohibited outdoor grilling at restaurants.

Serves 8

1 leg of lamb, butterflied
3 large lemons
4 large cloves garlic, minced
2 t. chopped fresh (or 1 t. dried) thyme leaves
1 t. dried oregano
1 t. chopped fresh (or 1/2 t. dried) rosemary
black pepper
1 c. olive oil
salt

Have your butcher butterfly the lamb leg and trim the fat, leaving enough membrane to hold it together while cooking. Score the thicker places with a knife.

Carefully peel the lemons so as to remove only the yellow portion of the rind. Chop the rind into pieces about the size of a match head. Place the chopped rind in a medium mixing bowl. Add the juice of the 3 lemons, garlic, herbs, and a generous amount of freshly ground black pepper and mix together. Add olive oil and whisk well. In a shallow pan, pour the marinade over the lamb. Refrigerate and marinate for at least 4 hours and up to several days, turning periodically and basting the lamb with the marinade.

When ready to cook, bring the lamb to room temperature. Remove from marinade, sprinkle with salt, and grill over medium-hot heat for 12 minutes on each side. Cut off the thinner pieces after 8 minutes, turning those to cook 8 minutes on the other side.

Serve with white bean casserole (page 43) or white bean purée (page 44) and ratatouille (page 41).

Braised Pork with Bourbon and Prunes

Bill was a great fan of Simone Beck, friend and collaborator of Julia Child. This recipe adapted from *Simca's Cuisine* was a great crowd pleaser on winter nights in the early days of La Res.

Serves 6

3 lbs. pork loin, in one piece, boned and tied
18 prunes
2 c. or more beef bouillon
1/2 c. Dijon mustard
2/3 c. dark brown sugar
2 T. peanut or vegetable oil
2/3 c. bourbon
salt and pepper to taste
bouquet garni of thyme, sage, and parsley
1 t. cornstarch, mixed with 2 T. water or bouillon
1 bunch watercress

Preheat oven to 375°.

Steep the prunes in about 1 c. of bouillon.

Wash the meat and pat dry with paper towels. Brush the meat with the mustard; then roll it in the brown sugar.

Heat the oil in a heavy ovenproof pot or Dutch oven and brown the meat on all sides. The sugar will caramelize; watch carefully to see that it does not burn.

Pour half of the whiskey over the meat and set it aflame. When the flame goes out, pour in 1/2 c. of the remaining bouillon, cover the pot, and place it in the preheated oven to cook for 1 hour and 25 minutes.

Halfway through the cooking, turn the meat, season with salt and pepper, add the bouquet garni, and lower the heat to 350°.

About 10 minutes before the end of the cooking time, add the prunes and their liquid.

Remove the meat to a warm platter, strain the cooking liquid, and remove the fat. Return the liquid to the pot, set over heat, and bring the sauce to the boil, adding the remaining whiskey and stirring to dislodge the sediments. Reduce the heat to medium. Stir the cornstarch to combine with the liquid and whisk into the sauce. Taste and correct the seasoning.

Slice half of the pork and present it on the serving dish with the unsliced pork. Ladle the sauce onto the platter and garnish with the prunes and watercress.

Sweetbreads with Capers and Brown Butter

Temptingly named sweetbreads, actually calves' thymus glands, are easy to love. Even innard-phobes will fall for the delicate flavor and texture of this delectable dish. Like the best French chefs, Bill wanted to use all the edible parts of a butchered animal. Brains and tripe—not surprisingly—failed to captivate our patrons, but this particular dish, with its combination of crunchy outside, soft inside, and tangy sauce, acquired an enthusiastic following.

Serves 4

1 1/2 lbs. veal sweetbreads
1 T. lemon juice
1/2 t. salt
2 eggs, beaten
1/2 c. fine bread crumbs
12 T. butter
3 T. lemon juice
4 T. small capers
chopped parsley

Soak the sweetbreads in water overnight. Drain and rinse. Place the sweetbreads in a saucepan. Cover with cold water seasoned with lemon juice and salt. Bring to a boil and simmer for 1 minute. Remove from heat, drain, and rinse under cold water. Remove the membranes, sinews, and excess fat. Place the sweetbreads on a cookie sheet lined with wax paper. Cover with wax paper and another cookie sheet and place several heavy objects on top of the cookie sheet to press the sweetbreads. Press, refrigerated, for several hours or overnight.

When ready to serve, heat 4 T. of butter over medium-high heat. Dip the sweetbreads in the egg, then in the bread crumbs. Sauté until golden brown.

Remove the sweetbreads from the pan. Add the remaining butter and cook until light brown. Add the lemon juice and capers and immediately remove from heat.

Pour over the sweetbreads, garnish with parsley, and serve.

Sweetbreads Ecossaise

Though sweetbreads with brown butter and capers was the favorite of our thymus-loving patrons, occasionally we substituted this sinfully rich dish for variety. Though *écossaise* translates as "Scottish," I doubt that this dish shows up on restaurant menus anywhere near Edinburgh. "Ecossaise" was the staff's reference to Drambuie, a liqueur made from Scotch whiskey.

Serves 4

1/2 c. Drambuie
2 T. lemon juice
1 c. heavy cream
salt and pepper to taste
1 1/2 lb. sweetbreads, poached, cleaned, and pressed (see page 69)
flour
4 T. clarified butter
12 white mushrooms, quartered
2 T. chopped parsley

For the sauce, simmer the Drambuie and lemon juice in a small saucepan until reduced by half. Add the cream and reduce by half again. Season with salt and pepper and keep warm over low heat. Dust the sweetbreads with flour and sauté in 3 T. of the butter until golden brown, a few minutes on each side. Remove to a warm plate. Sauté the mushrooms in the remaining butter over high heat for a minute or two. Add the mushrooms and the parsley to the warm sauce and pour over the sweetbreads.

Veal Chops Italienne

Because of our use of veal, animal rights activists boycotted La Résidence in the late 1970s. Picketers actually marched in front of the restaurant, raising our consciousness about the use of white milk-fed veal. We responded by substituting Chatham County free-range veal until some veal-loving patrons launched their own counter-protest.

The meat of those happier young free-range calves turned out to be just too dark and strongly flavored for Bill's subtle *blanquette de veau*. Bill solved the veal problem with this dish, creating a sauce strong enough to enhance the more beefy-tasting meat. The sauce works with chicken and scallops as well, and will keep nicely for several days in the refrigerator.

Serves 4 to 6

3/4 c. extra virgin olive oil
1 1/2 lbs. sliced mushrooms
5 cloves garlic, minced
1/4 c. chopped canned anchovies
2 T. capers
2 T. lemon juice
salt and pepper to taste
4–6 thick veal chops
3 T. chopped parsley

Sauté the mushrooms and garlic in olive oil until soft. Add the anchovies and stir until they dissolve into the oil. Take off the heat and stir in the capers and lemon juice. Set aside. Pan-grill the veal chops to desired doneness. Pour the mushrooms and sauce into the pan to warm. Serve the veal with sauce and mushrooms spooned on top. Sprinkle with parsley.

Osso Bucco

Here is another veal dish, quite popular at La Res, which does not require delicate milk-fed veal. This recipe, close to the traditional Northern Italian version, is usually paired with risotto Milanese. We served the stew without the risotto, but sprinkled it heavily with gremolata, accompanied by crusty bread to soak up the braising liquid.

Serves 6

6 large veal shanks
1/2 c. flour
1 t. salt
1/2 t. black pepper
1/3 c. olive oil
1 1/2 c. chopped onions
2 peeled carrots, chopped
2 stalks celery, chopped
3 cloves garlic, minced
1 bay leaf
1 c. dry white wine
3 c. veal stock (substitute a mixture of chicken broth and beef broth)
1 14-oz. can diced tomatoes
grated peel of half an orange and half a lemon
2 t. dried thyme leaves
1 t. dried rosemary
salt and pepper to taste
gremolata (recipe follows)

Dredge the shanks in the flour mixed with salt and pepper. Heat half of the oil in a deep, heavy, wide-bottomed skillet with a lid. When the oil is hot, sear the veal chops until brown, about 3 minutes per side. Remove from the pan and set aside.

Add the remaining oil to the pan and sauté the onions, carrots, and celery for 3 minutes. Add the garlic and cook 5 or so minutes more until the vegetables are soft. Add the wine and simmer until the liquid is reduced by half its original volume. Add stock, tomatoes, citrus peels, herbs, salt, and pepper, and stir together.

Return the veal shanks to the pan, cover, and simmer over low heat for an hour and a half, stirring occasionally and turning the meat once or twice during the cooking process.

By this time the meat should be very tender, almost falling off the bone. If not, continue to braise another half hour or so. Let the meat rest for at least 15 minutes before serving. To serve, place each shank on a plate or a large shallow bowl. Ladle sauce on top and sprinkle each shank with gremolata.

Like most stews, osso bucco improves with age and can be made up to 2 or 3 days before serving.

GREMOLATA

grated peel of 1 lemon
2 t. minced fresh garlic
1/4 c. finely chopped parsley

Mix the ingredients together and use as a garnish.

Veal Kidneys with Mushrooms

Legendary UNC basketball coach Dean Smith was a regular patron of La Résidence by the time we moved to Rosemary Street in Chapel Hill. One night Bill experimented with veal kidneys for the "innard" spot on the menu usually occupied by the more popular sweetbreads. Coach Smith boldly ordered *rognons de veau aux champignons* and loved them so much that he requested them each visit thereafter. Even when they weren't on the menu, we always kept an order of kidneys in the kitchen in case "the Dean" dropped by.

Serves 6

2 lbs. veal kidneys, peeled and cleaned of excess fat
2 c. buttermilk
6 slices bacon
4 shallots, chopped finely

1 14-oz. can diced tomatoes, including liquid
1/4 c. port
1 t. chopped fresh basil
1 t. finely chopped fresh marjoram
2 T. sugar
1 t. mustard seeds
salt and pepper to taste
1 lb. small white mushrooms, sliced
1/2 c. crème fraiche or sour cream

Slice the kidneys in half lengthwise and remove the strip of fat and gristle in the middle. Cut into thick slices horizontally. Marinate the kidneys in buttermilk for at least an hour.

Meanwhile, make the sauce. Cook the bacon until crisp and brown. Remove from the pan. Reserve all but 2 T. of the bacon fat. Sauté the shallots in the 2 T. bacon fat until soft. Add the undrained tomatoes, port, and seasonings and simmer on low heat for 20 minutes. Add a little water if the liquid evaporates too fast.

Drain the kidneys well. Pat dry. In another pan, sauté the kidneys in the remaining bacon fat over high heat for a few minutes on each side until brown. Remove the kidneys to a colander or sieve to drain.

Add the mushrooms to the pan and sauté for a minute or two until just soft.

Add the mushrooms to the sauce and bring to a simmer. Remove from heat and stir in crème fraiche or sour cream. Adjust seasoning. Arrange the kidneys on a warm serving platter and pour the sauce over the kidneys.

DESSERTS

Queen of Sheba Cake

During his graduate school years, Bill—home with the baby while I worked night shifts in the kitchen of Hope Valley Country Club—followed Julia Child's trail through *Mastering the Art of French Cooking*. By this time we were catering parties on weekends. Between the two of us, I was the dessert specialist; Bill concentrated on the savories.

One day Bill heard about a part-time cooking job at Chapel Hill Country Club. There was just one small problem — the job called for a baker. Bill interviewed and got the job, having convinced the chef he had the necessary experience. Luckily, the job started in two weeks, during which time Bill learned to bake like a pro.

This French gâteau, a Julia Child classic, was his favorite chocolate dessert, and, along with my grandmother's vanity cake, he made it every week at Chapel Hill Country Club. Later we served Queen of Sheba cake at La Résidence when it first opened.

Serves 8 to 12

11 oz. semisweet chocolate
1 oz. bitter chocolate
6 T. dark rum
3 sticks unsalted butter
2 c. sugar
1/2 t. salt
1 t. almond extract
9 egg yolks
2 c. sifted flour
1 c. ground almonds, pulverized in a blender or food processor
9 egg whites
chocolate butter cream (recipe follows)

Preheat oven to 325°.

In a saucepan over low heat, melt the chocolate in the rum, stirring to mix. Set aside to cool to room temperature.

Cream the butter and sugar. Add the salt, almond extract, egg yolks, and then the cooled chocolate. Stir in the flour mixed with almonds. Mix thoroughly without beating.

Whip the egg whites with a pinch of salt added until fluffy. Carefully fold the egg whites into the chocolate mixture.

Bake in a buttered and floured 8-inch round cake pan for 15 to 20 minutes. The middle should be slightly underdone. Cool 15 minutes before turning the cake carefully out of the pan.

When thoroughly cooled, spread with chocolate butter cream.

Serve at room temperature.

CHOCOLATE BUTTER CREAM

3 oz. semisweet chocolate
6 T. coffee
1 stick (1/2 c.) unsalted butter

Melt chocolate in the coffee over very low heat. Add butter, 1 T. at a time, stirring after each addition until smooth. When all the chocolate has been incorporated, spread the butter cream on the cake.

Tarte Tatin

A popular French bistro dessert, tarte tatin often appeared on the menu at Fearrington in those early days when there were no dessert choices and therefore no leftovers. The pie doesn't keep well—the crusts gets soggy a few hours after baking—so make this for company. Your guests will love you for it.

Serves 8

PIECRUST

1 1/4 c. all-purpose flour
1 T. sugar
1/4 t. salt
6 T. unsalted butter, cut into 1/2-inch slices
1 large egg yolk
2 to 3 T. ice water

Pulse flour, sugar, and salt in food processor. Add butter and pulse 4 to 5 times, until mixture resembles coarse crumbs. Add egg yolk and pulse to blend. Add water; pulse until mixture just begins to come together. Shape pastry into a ball and flatten into a disk. Wrap and refrigerate 30 minutes or more.

CARAMEL

1/4 c. water

1/2 c. sugar

Bring the water and sugar to a boil in a small saucepan over medium-high heat. Cook, swirling the pan, until the syrup turns dark amber. Quickly pour caramel into a 9 1/2-inch deep-dish glass pie plate, tilting the plate so the bottom is evenly coated. Set aside.

FILLING

4 T. butter

1/3 c. sugar

5–6 cooking apples, peeled, cored, and quartered

Melt the butter in a 12-inch nonstick skillet. Add the sugar and cook 2 minutes. Add the apples and cook, gently stirring, until they are almost tender and lightly caramelized, 25 to 30 minutes.

Heat oven to 375°. Let the apples cool slightly in the pan. With a spoon, arrange apples cut-side up in 2 layers on top of the caramel.

Roll the pastry into an 11-inch circle; place on top of the apples. Fold up overhanging pastry along the rim of the pie plate. Bake until the pastry is golden brown and the filling is bubbly, about 35 minutes.

Let the tart cool on a rack for just 10 minutes. Invert a plate on top of the pie plate. Carefully invert the tart onto the plate. (If any of the apple pieces stick to the pie plate, carefully remove them with a small knife and put them back on the pastry.)

Kalouga

Is there anyone who doesn't love a soufflé after a big dinner? It melts in your mouth, slides effortlessly down the throat, and miraculously doesn't seem to add to an already full stomach. The problem with a soufflé is the perfect timing it requires in order to arrive at the table at the peak of warmth and airiness. Kalouga is the solution. This chocolate soufflé cake can be made up to a day ahead, and is still good, though somewhat denser, by the second day.

The mysteriously named Kalouga (named after a region in Russia, though its origin appears to be Burgundian) was the most popular dessert we ever served. It still appears on the menu at La Résidence after all these years.

Serves 8 to 12

10 1/2 oz. good semisweet chocolate (we used a Dutch brand called Peterson's)
1/4 c. brandy
1 3/4 stick (14 oz.) butter
2 c. cake flour
2 c. granulated sugar
1 t. salt
7 eggs, separated
1/2 c. sugar

Over low heat, melt together the chocolate, brandy, and butter. Cool to room temperature. Mix the flour, sugar, and salt together and stir into chocolate mixture. Beat the egg yolks until fluffy and light colored. Stir into the chocolate mixture.

Beat egg whites until foamy, gradually add sugar and continue beating until soft peaks are formed. Fold lightly into chocolate mixture, being careful not to overfold—a few streaks won't hurt.

Pour into greased and floured 9 1/2-inch round springform pan. Bake at 375° for 1/2 hour. Be careful not to overcook. This cake should be soft, even slightly runny in the middle. Serve with sweetened whipped cream, crème anglaise (page 82), or espresso ice cream (page 83).

Chocolate Roulade

When we opened La Résidence, many locals believed our silent partner was "the old professor" himself, Kay Kyser, the band leader and movie star. Not true, but without the moral support and aesthetic guidance of Kay's wife Georgia and daughter Carroll, La Res would have been an entirely different place.

The Kysers gave us this ethereal recipe, a family favorite and a tradition at their annual Christmas carol sing. We offered it on the dessert menu until Kalouga usurped its place, not because Kalouga tastes better, but because this roulade is very delicate and gets a bit soggy a day after making.

This flourless cake, really a soufflé, is prone to break as you roll it. Even if it falls apart, try to patch it back together. It's worth the effort.

Serves 10 to 12

CAKE

8 oz. semisweet chocolate
1/3 c. strong coffee
8 egg yolks, at room temperature
1 c. sugar
8 egg whites, at room temperature
1/4 t. salt
1/2 c. unsweetened cocoa

Preheat oven to 350°.

Cut 2 pieces of parchment paper to fit a 13 x 18 x 1-inch jelly roll pan. Grease one sheet of the paper with shortening or butter. Sprinkle with flour, shake off excess flour. Set aside the second sheet for later use.

In a saucepan, melt the chocolate in the coffee over low heat. Stir together until smooth. Let cool to room temperature.

In a medium-sized mixing bowl, beat the egg yolks with an electric mixer, while gradually adding the sugar, until fluffy and light in color. Fold the chocolate mixture thoroughly into the egg yolks using a rubber spatula.

With clean, dry beaters, beat the egg whites and salt until stiff, but without forming dry peaks. Lightly fold about 1/4 of the whites into the yolk mixture. Then fold the rest of the whites into the yolk mixture, careful not to overblend.

Gently pour into prepared jelly roll pan and level off. Bake at 350° for 15 to 18 minutes or until set.

Place the pan on cooling rack. After 5 minutes, sift the cocoa evenly onto the top of the cake. Immediately place the second sheet of parchment paper onto the top of the cocoa-sprinkled roulade and carefully flip the cake upside down. Remove the pan and slowly peel off the bottom sheet of parchment.

Roll up the long side of the cake—the paper will now be on the inside of the roll. Allow the cake to cool in this position while you make the filling.

FILLING

1 1/2 c. whipping cream
1/4 c. sugar
1 t. vanilla
1 t. bourbon or cognac

Whip the cream, gradually adding 1/4 c. sugar, until stiff peaks form. Beat in the vanilla and bourbon (or cognac) and refrigerate.

When the cake reaches room temperature, gently unroll the cake and peel off the paper. Spread the filling evenly onto the cake. Roll the cake back up lengthwise, and sprinkle the top with more cocoa. Chill for at least 1 hour before slicing with a knife dipped in hot water.

This dessert should be served within a few hours of making.

Walnut Roulade

This is the richest and the most versatile of all of the roulades served at La Résidence. We served it on request for special occasions. Presented on a long, narrow platter and decorated with whipped cream swirls, it makes a striking presentation. Like chocolate roulade, it should be eaten within a few hours of having been made.

Serves 8 to 12

8 egg yolks
1 c. sugar
8 egg whites
1/4 t. salt
2 c. ground walnuts
1 1/2 t. baking powder
1 c. sifted powdered sugar
mocha or fruit filling (recipes follow)

Preheat oven to 350°.

Line a jelly roll pan with greased and floured parchment paper.

In a mixing bowl beat together the sugar and egg yolks until light colored and fluffy. Beat the egg whites with the salt until stiff peaks form.

Stir the baking powder into the walnuts, mixing evenly. Fold the walnuts into the egg yolks, then gently fold in the whites. Spread the mixture onto the prepared pan.

Bake for about 25 to 30 minutes or until firm in the middle.

Remove the pan from the oven and immediately sprinkle the top of the cake lightly with powdered sugar. The sugar should evenly cover the cake.

Carefully invert the cake onto a new sheet of parchment paper cut big enough to cover the cake. Cool. Then peel away the parchment from what is now the top of the cake.

When the cake has cooled to room temperature, spread with mocha or fruit filling. Carefully roll up the cake from the longer side, peeling off the remaining parchment paper as you roll.

Serve with extra whipped cream or powdered sugar sprinkled on top.

MOCHA FILLING

2 c. heavy cream
1/4 c. sugar
1 t. instant coffee dissolved in 2 T. rum

Whip the cream adding the sugar as you beat, until stiff peaks form. Stir in the dissolved coffee, blending well. Be careful not to beat too much or the cream will curdle.

FRUIT FILLING

2 c. heavy cream
1/4 c. sugar
2 T. Grand Marnier or rum
sliced strawberries or peaches

Whip the cream adding the sugar as you beat. Stir in Grand Marnier or rum and fold in sliced peaches or strawberries in season.

Crème Anglaise

Our grandmothers used this simple dessert sauce, referred to as boiled custard in the South, as a tonic for the sick. The ultimate comfort food, it's irresistible even when nothing else will stimulate the appetite.

In France it is often served as a complement to a soufflé, another great comfort food.

Makes 1 qt.

3 c. milk
1 c. sugar
8 egg yolks
pinch of salt
1/4 c. heavy cream
1 t. vanilla

Heat the milk in a heavy nonreactive saucepan until it steams and forms a scum on top, but don't let it boil.

Meanwhile, whisk the yolks, sugar, and pinch of salt until the mixture is pale yellow. Slowly pour the hot milk into the yolks, beating all the while, and pour the mixture back unto the saucepan.

Over very low heat, cook the mixture, stirring constantly until it thickens or coats a spoon. Immediately take the pan off heat. Add the vanilla and the cream, to prevent the custard from curdling.

Chill immediately.

Honey Chocolate Sauce

Here is a chocolate sundae sauce with a difference. We served it over our homemade vanilla ice cream accompanied by brown-edged wafers (page 93).

Makes 2 1/2 c.

1 c. heavy cream
pinch of salt
4 oz. unsweetened chocolate
4 oz. semisweet chocolate
1 c. honey
grated rind of 2 oranges
1/2 c. rum, dark or light

Over moderate heat bring to a boil the cream, salt, chocolates, and honey, stirring often. Turn the heat to low and simmer for 2 to 3 minutes without stirring. Remove from heat and stir in the orange rind. When cool, stir in the rum. Serve over vanilla or banana ice cream.

Espresso Ice Cream

Occasionally, we would receive a call from a disgruntled customer who complained, "The waiter must have served us caffeinated coffee instead of the decaf we asked for. We couldn't sleep all night!" When asked what this patron had for dessert, the answer invariably was "espresso ice cream."

Our recipe comes with a warning: eat with caution. This ice cream is perfect to consume when studying for exams or after a heavy lunch, but maybe not before bedtime.

For those of you daring enough to risk a major caffeine buzz, try espresso ice cream with a slice of warm Kalouga.

Makes 1 1/2 qts.

La Résidence ice cream base (recipe follows)
2 T. instant espresso dissolved in a little water
1/3 c. Kahlua
1/4 c. coarsely ground espresso beans (not instant)

LA RÉSIDENCE ICE CREAM BASE

This is the richest ice cream imaginable. If the high-fat content of this recipe scares you, substitute half-and-half for the heavy cream and butter—but the egg yolks are essential.

1 3/4 c. half-and-half
2 t. vanilla extract
9 egg yolks
3/4 c. sugar
1/4 t. salt
6 T. unsalted butter
1 1/2 c. heavy cream

Scald the half-and-half mixed with the vanilla extract. Beat the egg yolks, sugar, and salt in a mixing bowl until well blended, but not fluffy. Gradually beat the hot cream into the egg mixture.

In a thick-bottomed saucepan, cook over very low heat until the mixture thickens enough to coat a spoon. Take immediately off the heat to prevent curdling, and add the butter and the cold cream right away.

Stir in the dissolved instant espresso and Kahlua. Refrigerate the mixture until chilled.

Freeze in an ice cream maker until almost stiff. Stop the machine and add the ground espresso beans at this point. Continue to churn a few more minutes. Pour into a container and allow to ripen up in the freezer for at least an hour before serving.

Fig Ice Cream with Port

Like persimmon pudding at Crook's, fig ice cream would appear on the menu at La Res very briefly, as the ripe fruit became available in late summer. We kept a list of patrons who asked to be called as soon as this eagerly anticipated dessert appeared on the menu.

Makes 1 1/2 qts.

La Résidence ice cream base (page 84), omitting the butter
1 1/2 c. mashed figs sprinkled with 1 t. lemon juice
ruby port

Stir the fig purée into the chilled custard base. Freeze in an ice cream freezer. Serve in a footed coupe or wide-mouthed wineglass topped with ruby port.

Galliano Chocolate-Chunk Ice Cream

In a remote part of Southern France, we visited Chartreuse, where monks have made the herbaceous green-yellow liqueur of that name for centuries. Bill loved its complex flavor, and the history of the Carthusian order fascinated him. We searched for Chartreuse and other liqueurs when we got back home, and experimented with desserts flavored with our favorites. These desserts, usually ice creams, had great appeal to diners who would have enjoyed a digestif—Benedictine, Armagnac, or Grand Marnier—had such liqueurs been allowed in dry Chatham County. We made periodic trips to Washington to stock up on these "flavorings," which were legal to use in desserts but not to drink.

On a later trip to Florence, I tasted a cake similar to Boston cream pie with a vaguely Chartreuse-like liqueur added to the custard. This combination of Strega (Italian for "the witch") and chocolate was too good not to use in an ice cream. We ended up substituting almost-as-bewitching Galliano, available locally. This became one of Bill's favorite desserts. If you come across a bottle of "the witch," it is sure to cast a spell over you.

Makes 1 1/2 qts.

La Résidence ice cream base (page 84)
1/2 c. Galliano or Strega liqueur
6 oz. semisweet chocolate, broken into rough chunks

Stir the liqueur into the ice cream base before freezing. When the ice cream begins to freeze and thicken, stop the ice cream maker and add the chocolate chunks. Continue freezing until very thick.

Ginger Ice Cream

In the early stages of the nouvelle cuisine trend in the 1970s, Bill and I visited Washington to explore the hottest new restaurants. Although Lyon d'Or and Jean-Claude's were impressive, our favorite was not classic French but instead Vietnamese—Germaine's. This popular Georgetown eatery reflected the former French occupation of Vietnam and was ahead of its time in offering Asian flavors with Gallic flair. For dessert there, we ordered a French-style *glacé* flavored with fresh ginger. We were so impressed that we tried to re-create it at La Résidence. Sometimes we served it with an apple or pear tart, but it is sublime just by itself.

Serves 4

2 c. half-and-half
2 T. finely chopped fresh ginger
1/2 c. sugar
pinch salt
3 egg yolks
3 T. chopped candied ginger (optional)

In a stainless steel saucepan, heat the cream to the simmering point. Cut off the heat and add the chopped ginger. Let the ginger steep in the hot cream for 30 minutes.

Lightly whisk the egg yolks with sugar and a tiny pinch of salt. Pour the cream through a strainer to remove the ginger. Reheat the cream just to the boiling point. Slowly pour the hot cream into the egg mixture while whisking lightly. When well blended, place the pan over very low heat (or in the top of a double boiler over simmering water) and stir the mixture constantly until it custardizes, or coats a spoon.

Immediately remove from heat and place the saucepan in a bowl of cold water to stop the cooking process. Allow to cool until it reaches room temperature; then refrigerate to chill.

Freeze in an ice cream machine. Serve topped with chopped candied ginger if you like.

Honey Thyme Ice Cream

The move to Rosemary Street in 1978 initiated an era of expansion for La Résidence. No longer could the entire staff gather around one table before the evening shift. Bill kept in touch with his growing number of employees at a potluck lunch that became a monthly ritual. Each staff member was encouraged to bring a dish appropriate to use on the menu. Bill would award a bottle of champagne to the person who brought the best dish.

This contribution, a Provençal recipe discovered by dessert cook Barbara Tolley, was the hands-down winner at one of these lively summer lunches on the porch.

Serves 4 to 6

6 T. honey
1/4 c. water
1 T. fresh thyme leaves
4 egg yolks
2 c. half-and-half

In a small saucepan, bring to a boil the thyme, honey, and water. Simmer over low heat for 1 minute. Let sit for about 10 minutes before pouring the liquid through a sieve to strain the thyme leaves out. If the honey mixture has thickened too much to pour easily, reheat slightly, strain, and cool to room temperature.

Beat the egg yolks slightly. Add the honey mixture. In a heavy nonreactive saucepan, heat the half-and-half until it steams. Gradually pour the hot cream into the egg mixture, stirring constantly. Pour this mixture back into the saucepan. Cook over very low heat, stirring constantly until the custard thickens. Immediately remove from heat, pour into a bowl, and refrigerate until cold. Freeze in an ice cream maker.

Caramel Mousse

The recipe for this simple frozen mousse came from my father, Henry Hobbs, a creative cook, warm host, and friend and mentor of Bill.

Serves 8

8 egg yolks
2 1/2 c. cream, whipped
1 1/4 c. water
1 1/3 c. sugar
1 t. vanilla
sweetened whipped cream
candied violets or sugared pecans

Beat egg yolks until thick and lemon colored. Whip the cream until soft peaks form. Boil 1/2 c. plus 1 T. water in a saucepan or in the microwave.

Hold at a simmer while heating, in a heavy saucepan, the sugar and the remaining 3 T. of water to the boiling point, stirring occasionally.

Once the mixture boils, continue to cook without stirring until the mixture begins to caramelize. Watch carefully and remove from heat when it is medium brown. Immediately pour the boiling water slowly into the caramel. This will stop the caramel from darkening any further and thin it somewhat.

Very gradually whip the caramel syrup into the egg yolks, beating until the mixture thickens again. Add vanilla. Fold in the whipped cream until the mousse is smooth and evenly colored.

Spoon into individual 4- to 5-oz. timbales or soufflé dishes. Freeze. Serve topped with sweetened whipped cream. We garnished the dollop of whipped cream with a single candied violet on top.

Chocolate Mousse

We thought all restaurants based on French cuisine should offer chocolate mousse. This was ours.

Serves 6 to 8

1 T. instant coffee
1/3 c. boiling water
6 oz. semisweet chocolate, broken into chunks
1 T. cognac or brandy
1 t. vanilla
5 eggs at room temperature
1/2 c. heavy cream
pinch of salt
sweetened whipped cream
chocolate shavings

Dissolve the coffee in the boiling water in a medium-sized saucepan. Add the chocolate chunks. Stir gently, over very low heat, until the chocolate is melted and the mixture is smooth. Stir in the vanilla and cognac. Allow the mixture to cool until room temperature.

Separate the eggs into 2 large bowls.

Beat the egg yolks until light and lemon colored. Fold the yolks into the chocolate.

Whip the cream until thick.

Whip the egg whites with salt and cream of tartar until stiff peaks form. Fold the whites and the cream lightly into the chocolate mixture. Pour into wine glasses or ramekins and refrigerate until cold. We garnished our mousse with a dollop of sweetened whipped cream and chocolate shavings.

Lemon Mousse

For a bridesmaid luncheon at La Résidence in the late 1970s, the mother of the bride requested for dessert, "Something light and pretty, say, a lemon mousse." Eager to please, I agreed to make a lemon mousse, though I'd never tasted such a thing. The solution was to lighten the lemon curd we kept on hand for cakes and roulades with whipped cream. The bridal party happily gobbled up every bite.

We liked it so much, we added it to the dessert menu. Later Bill lightened it further with beaten egg whites and served it at Crook's. You can still find it on the menu there each summer, served with fresh sweet blueberries.

Serves 4 to 6

1 recipe lemon curd (recipe follows)
1 1/2 c. whipping cream
2 egg whites, whipped to soft peaks (optional)
fresh blueberries or other fruit (optional)
sweetened whipped cream
toasted almonds (optional)

Make the lemon curd.

Whip the cream to soft peaks. Carefully fold the curd into the whipped cream. Spoon into serving bowls or wine glasses. For a lighter mousse, fold the egg whites into the lemon curd before folding in the whipped cream.

This mousse is delicious by itself or with strawberries, blueberries, or blackberries. Serve topped with a dollop of whipped cream. If you'd like to add a crunchy texture, sprinkle toasted almonds on top of the cream.

LEMON CURD

In England, lemon curd is used commonly as a spread for toast. It also makes a lovely filling for yellow cake or meringue shells.

1 c. white sugar
4 egg yolks
1/3 c. lemon juice

1 T. *grated lemon rind*
4 T. *butter*

Using a whisk, mix together the first 4 ingredients until well blended but not frothy. In a heavy-bottomed saucepan over low heat, stir the mixture constantly until it thickens, or custardizes. At this point it should be steaming hot, but not boiling. Immediately take the pan off the heat and add the butter, 1 T. at a time, stirring until well blended.

Grand Marnier Sabayon

After a rich meal, there's always room for this smooth, elegant pudding. The recipe was one of many introduced to France when Florentine Catherine de Medici married Henry II. Although usually served hot without the addition of whipped cream, our version can be made ahead and refrigerated for hours. In Italy sabayon, called *zabaglione*, is traditionally made with the dessert wine Marsala. Grand Marnier makes it just a little grander.

Serves 4 to 6

4 *egg yolks*
1/2 *c. sugar*
1/3 *c. plus 1 1/2 T. Grand Marnier*
3/4 *c. whipping cream*

Place the egg yolks, sugar, and 1/3 c. Grand Marnier in a stainless steel bowl or the top of a double boiler. With a hand mixer, beat together the ingredients. Meanwhile, heat an inch of water in a saucepan or the lower part of the boiler. Place the container of the egg mixture over the simmering water and beat until the mixture is thick, light yellow, and steaming. Remove from heat and refrigerate to bring to room temperature or cooler.

Whip the cream and add the remaining Grand Marnier at the last minute, careful not to beat too much and cause the cream to curdle. Fold the cream into the cool egg mixture. Serve with fresh fruit—strawberries, peaches, blueberries, blackberries—or simply by itself.

Blackberry Sorbet

La Res always offered at least one sorbet for folks who wanted a light dessert. Because a purée of frozen blackberries is almost as good as one made from fresh berries, this sorbet is delicious any season of the year.

Serves 8 to 10

3 1/2 c. purée of fresh or frozen blackberries, strained to get the seeds out
1 1/2 c. sugar syrup
1/4 c. triple sec
5 T. gin
1 T. lemon juice

Mix all of the ingredients and freeze in an ice cream maker.

Passion Fruit Sorbet

This simple sorbet was a favorite on the Valentine's Day menu. You can substitute mango or papaya for a less romantic, but just as tasty, dessert.

Serves 8 to 10

2 c. fresh or frozen passion fruit purée
2 T. lime juice
1/2 c. light rum
2 c. simple syrup (recipe follows)

Mix together and freeze in an ice cream maker.

SIMPLE SYRUP

1 1/2 c. sugar
1 1/2 c. water

In a saucepan, stir water and sugar together. Bring to a boil and simmer for 1 minute. Remove from heat and chill.

Fresh Fruit with Mint and Lillet

We kept this simple fruit salad on the dessert menu for diners who were just too full for a rich dessert. It also makes a lovely first course for lunch or brunch.

ripe melon of your choice
berries in season
peaches, plums, or other juicy-fleshed fruit of your choice
finely chopped fresh mint
Lillet Blanc

Cut the melon and other fruit into fairly uniform cubes. Add berries and mint. Sprinkle with Lillet and toss gently. For dessert, serve in a pretty bowl with brown-edged wafers (next recipe) or shortbread on the side.

Brown-Edged Wafers

These may be the best cookies on earth. Certainly they're among the easiest to make. I noticed in Julia Child's recently published *Kitchen Wisdom* a recipe for a similar type of cookie called *langues de chat*. She must agree with me because it's the only cookie recipe in the book.

Long before I'd heard of Julia, I spent many afternoons with high school friends making these cookies. We ate so much of the dough that we had hardly any left for the finished product. Bill baked thousands of brown-edged wafers for the Chapel Hill Country Club, and we gave them to friends in Christmas baskets every year.

Ben and Karen Barker, who graced La Résidence's kitchen in the 1980s, still serve them with Karen's exquisite ice creams and sorbets at their acclaimed Durham restaurant, Magnolia Grill.

At least 2 dozen cookies

1 c. salted butter (or unsalted with a liberal pinch of salt added)
1 c. sugar

2 egg whites
1 1/2 c. flour

Cream the butter. Gradually beat in the sugar, blending until fluffy. Add the unbeaten egg whites, one at a time, blending well. Do not overbeat. Stir in the flour. Drop by teaspoons on an ungreased cookie sheet, at least 2 inches apart.

Bake at 350° until just brown around the edges, about 10 minutes or less.

Cool for about a minute before removing with a spatula, working fast before cookies cool completely, or they will crumble when lifted.

BEVERAGES

Cocktail La Res

By 1978 La Res had moved to Chapel Hill from its home in dry Chatham County. Coincidentally "liquor by the drink" had just passed in an Orange County referendum. So delighted were we to be able to offer wine in the restaurant that we didn't bother to acquire a liquor license until the following year. But once we committed to selling the hard stuff, we wanted to emulate restaurants in France by coming up with an *apéritif de maison*. Cocktail La Res was the result, a European-style "wet" martini. If you can't find Lillet, substitute Dubonnet or another brand of sweet vermouth, either white or red.

For one drink

1 part gin
2 parts Lillet Blanc
2 parts dry vermouth
twist of orange peel

French 75

On a recent wedding anniversary, my husband Drake treated me to an extravagant dinner at a fine local dining establishment. After we were seated, our waiter asked if we would care for an aperitif. I responded, "Yes, I'd like a French 75." Our waiter's eyebrows rose as he announced, "I'll have to get the wine steward to help you with that." A little puzzled, we waited as another fellow approached our table. "We don't have a '75," the wine steward apologized, "but we have a delicious '63."

After we stopped laughing, the realization set in that the French 75, named for a French 75-millimeter gun, hasn't yet undergone a revival in this neo-cocktail age. I think it's time to change that.

In New Orleans, French 75s have never gone out of style in the older restaurants of the French Quarter. Bill and I both loved this cocktail and served it at La Résidence once serving liquor in restaurants became legal.

For one drink

1 1/4 oz. gin
1 t. sugar
1 oz. lemon juice
dry champagne or sparkling wine

Pour the gin, lemon juice, and sugar into a cocktail shaker filled with 3 ice cubes. Shake and strain into a chilled champagne glass. Fill the glass with champagne and enjoy.

La Résidence Coffee Blend

This particular blend of coffee beans from Broad Street Coffee Roasters in Durham is still used at La Résidence. The blend is available from other coffee vendors, but you can make it at home with this combination of beans:

1 part Sumatran blend, medium roast
1 part Ethiopian blend, medium roast
2 parts Vienna Roast blend (a very dark roast blend)

Crook's Corner

APPETIZERS AND SOUPS
Pimento Cheese and Crackers
Artichokes with Goat Cheese and Mustard Vinaigrette
Crab Soup
Garlic Soup with Mushrooms
Marmite Provençale
Mediterranean Vegetable Soup
Oriental Mushroom Soup
White Bean Soup

BREADS
Black Pepper Cornbread
Jalapeño Hushpuppies

CONDIMENTS AND SAUCES
Crook's Corner Cajun Salt
Crook's Corner Creole Mustard
Curry Spice Mix
Blue Cheese Dressing
Crook's House Dressing
Green and Gold Dressing

Herb Vinaigrette
Yogurt Basil Vinaigrette
Crook's House Mayonnaise
Cocktail Sauce
Tartar Sauce
Crook's Tomato Sauce

SIDE DISHES
Cheese Grits
Dirty Rice
Hoppin' John
Curried Peaches
Stuffed Sweet Potatoes
Whipped Potatoes
Red Slaw

MAIN COURSES
Catfish in Creole Sauce
Mussels Marinière
Broiled Oysters
Salmon with Pebbly Mustard Sauce
Maque Choux with Shrimp
Shrimp and Grits
Trout with Bacon and Scallions
Chicken Country Captain
Chicken Livers with Mushrooms
Wonderful Meatballs

Braised Pork Chops with Baby Limas and Whole Garlic
Country-Style Roast Ribs
Cajun Steak
Mustard Lover's Steak

DESSERTS
Crook's Hot Fudge Brownies
Mount Airy Chocolate Soufflé Cake
Huguenot Torte
Caramel Ice Cream
Vanilla Ice Cream
Pear Cranberry Pie
Bourbon Pecan Pie
Princess Pamela's Buttermilk Pie
Sweet Potato Pie
Bread Pudding
Persimmon Pudding

In this venue Bill resuscitated the diminishing art of southern cuisines,
emphasizing the South Carolina Lowcountry, and the Louisiana bayou, and
adding dishes from all over the South. The menu, like a freshly improvised
old jazz standard, is traditional southern — but its nouvelle-inspired
flexibility allows creative musings on those old themes.
Matt Jones, Spectator Magazine

Eating dinner at Crook's is like coming home.
Lee Smith

he original Crook's Corner, built in 1941 at the juncture of Chapel Hill and Carrboro, was the site of Rachel Crook's fish and vegetable market. After the fatal shooting of Mrs. Crook, a mystery unsolved to this day, the space was occupied by a taxi stand, and later a pool hall. By 1978 the building had fallen into a state of pretty drastic disrepair. Cam Hill, a popular builder who lived in the neighborhood, recognized its potential as a gathering place and came to the rescue. He renovated the dilapidated building and reopened it as a beer and barbecue joint, which quickly became a neighborhood hangout. A regular clientele largely made up of auto mechanics, construction workers, and UNC dropouts congregated there after work, drinking beer and playing poker until the wee hours of the morning.

Four years later Cam offered his buddies Bill Neal and Gene Hamer a chance to lease the place to start a "real" restaurant. Cam's entourage, affectionately called "the lost boys" by Bill, with just a hint of envy, was none too pleased with the prospect.

Gene described opening night of the new Crook's in 1982: "We were scheduled to open at six, but to our horror, at five o'clock the regulars showed up. They filled up the tables, pulled out their playing cards, and proceeded to make themselves at home. They were protesting the change to a more upscale scene by staging a sit-in! I said to Bill, 'Holy Hell, what are we going to do? They're not going to leave all night.' Fifteen minutes before opening Bill took action. 'Go out and tell them that whoever is going to eat can stay. The rest have to move to the bar or go outside.' I was sure they wouldn't budge, but thankfully most did, although some stayed for fifteen minutes or so to save face. Many of these guys came back to the bar for years. There was one, an extremely skinny mechanic, who only ordered drinks, no food. Bill worried about his health, and every time this fellow came to the bar, he would send him a plate of vegetables."

During Crook's early years, Bill was still cooking primarily in the Euro-centric style of La Résidence. One day in 1984, Craig Claiborne showed up in Chapel Hill to research an article on Southern food for the New York Times. Bill was invited to lead this powerful tastemaker on a tour of barbecue joints in small Eastern North Carolina towns. At the time the country was California-crazy, with such restaurants as Alice Waters's Chez Panisse and Jeremiah Towers's Stars attracting a lot of attention. After spending time with Mr. Claiborne, a Mississippian by birth, Bill found that his vision began to come into focus. "The South has at least as much as California to offer," he told Mr. Claiborne. Bill envisioned a niche that nobody had filled, and he moved in that direction.

Bill left Crook's for a year to concentrate on writing the book that became Bill Neal's Southern Cooking. When he returned, the menu reflected his new direction, emphasizing Lowcountry, Carolina Piedmont, and Cajun dishes. Crab cakes, country captain, and Cajun rib eye appeared, and of course Bill's version of shrimp and grits, created especially for Mr. Claiborne when he re-turned for another visit. The ensuing New York Times article propelled Crook's into another realm. The popular local restaurant suddenly became a nation-ally known one. According to Gene, "After that article, Crook's boomed. Customers trekked in from all over the state and beyond."

Though the restaurant became a magnet for visiting celebrities, it still maintained its neighborhood ambience. "I remember the night Buckmin-ster Fuller came to eat before lecturing at UNC," recalls Gene. "Bill com-mented that he felt proud to have a place where a world-famous architect and ordinary construction workers could dine next to each other. Phyllis Richmond (restaurant critic of the Washington Post at the time) was a big fan of Bill's and tried to persuade us to move to D.C., but we had no interest in leaving Chapel Hill."

Crook's has become a model for several excellent eateries that have sprung up throughout the South, including Charleston's acclaimed Hominy Grill. Its owner, Robert Stehling, began his career as a dishwasher at Crook's. Robert credits Bill with changing the direction of his life: "Bill would cook something for the menu and ask [the staff] to respond to its taste. Was it exciting to eat? Were the flavors balanced? What could be done to improve it? All of us would discuss the dish, its history, and its place in Southern culture. This way of looking at food was so exciting to me and I learned so much, I ended up dropping out of UNC. I worked up to line cook, and eventually became kitchen manager when Bill left to write a book.

"Before coming to Charleston I spent eight years working in lots of different restaurants in New York. I missed the atmosphere at Crook's, where everyone in the kitchen was encouraged to learn as much as they could. That attitude just doesn't exist in the competitive atmosphere up north. In Chapel Hill Bill and Gene had a strong connection to the community and were committed to their employees, not just their ambitions.

"I modeled my cooking after Bill's — it's not about odd combinations or fancy presentation. In my mind, it's not restaurant cooking, it's home cooking. When I opened this place I thought of it as an extension of Crook's. I still use Bill's biscuit recipe with lard, his pimento cheese, and several of the basics straight out of Bill Neal's Southern Cooking. You just can't beat them."

John Currence, chef and owner of the James Beard Foundation–cited City Grocery in Oxford, Mississippi, also began his career in the kitchen at Crook's.

"I owe Bill for teaching me some things that have been vital to the way I run my restaurant here in Oxford. Bill used ingredients that had previously had a pedestrian connotation, such as collard greens and black-eyed peas. This was at a time when big chains like McDonald's were putting little country mom-and-pop places out of business. Real, true Southern cooking was becoming almost extinct. Bill raised the question, 'What is great American cooking?' and tried to bring it back.

"From Bill I gained an appreciation for freshness of ingredients that I didn't see when I moved on to other restaurants. He nurtured local produce growers. At Crook's I learned that you can run a restaurant and 'have a life.' Crook's was not about competition. It was part of the neighborhood."

About Bill's famous artistic temperament, he adds, "It's true I left Crook's after an unpleasant scene over acorn squash soup. And, yes, there was a coffee-throwing incident. But looking back, I owe Bill a lot. Southern Cooking was a primer for me about what good cooking should be, and also what he was about. Bill did have a temper, but he was an artist, a perfectionist, and cared tremendously about what he did."

"Bill came along when dining out in the South meant a trip to the steak house, a Chinese restaurant, or a country club," adds another former Crook's employee, Kevin Callahan, who now owns Acme Food and Beverage just down the road in Carrboro. "He was the first person I knew of to claim that Southern food, the kind served at family reunions, deserved respect. That attitude had an effect on what it meant to work in a restaurant. Bill showed us all that it was worthwhile work. Today we all stand on his shoulders."

For the past decade Bill Smith has presided over the kitchen at Crook's Corner, creating his own distinctive improvisations while preserving the best loved of Bill Neal's recipes. More literally than any other protégé of Bill Neal, Smith has followed in his footsteps, arriving at Crook's in 1992 after heading the kitchen at La Résidence for seven years.

"At Crook's I make most of the old standards people love to eat over and over again, but I put my own spin on some of the recipes," Smith says.

"Now 'seasonal' seems to be a more accurate description of the food we serve at Crook's. We have so many interesting fresh ingredients available now that can't really be classified as traditional Southern. Local farmers are growing pretty exotic things like fresh fennel and fava beans, and they make all kinds of wonderful goat cheeses. I still buy produce from the same farmers who have supplied Crook's and La Résidence for twenty years."

Asked what makes Crook's such a special place, Gene Hamer thoughtfully answered, "Basically we have had only two chefs in twenty years, and this gives a consistency to our food. Both Bill Neal and Bill Smith are very much respected and appreciated by the local community for their work.

"Nationally, Bill's books still give us a presence. People think they know him. To this day, more than ten years since he died, people still come in and ask to speak to Bill Neal." With characteristic modesty, Gene neglected to mention his own steady and unfailingly hospitable presence, one more reason Crook's feels like home to so many of its patrons.

APPETIZERS AND SOUPS

Pimento Cheese and Crackers

According to a statement of Bill's that I have in my notes, "Pimento cheese is the pâté of the South, a movable feast that goes to picnics, football games, and beach weekends. A grilled pimento cheese sandwich is a Southern drugstore classic that evokes as much debate as the topics of jambalaya and juleps. Everyone is fiercely loyal to one version or another; this one pleases the patrons of Crook's Corner."

You can find this same pimento cheese every night at Crook's, either on the Cracker Plate or the Dixie Plate.

Makes 3 c.

12 oz. aged white cheddar
1/3 c. grated Parmesan cheese
1/4 c. diced canned pimientos, drained
6 T. mayonnaise
1 1/2 t. bourbon
1/4 t. chili powder
1/8 t. freshly ground black pepper
1/8 t. ground cumin

Grate the cheddar by hand. Add the rest of the ingredients and stir lightly to mix. Refrigerate for 30 minutes before serving with crackers.

Artichokes with Goat Cheese and Mustard Vinaigrette

Not long after Crook's Corner opened, food writer Lou Seibert Pappas included Bill in her column "Great American Chefs," in which she described Crook's as "an American answer to a French bistro." Bill was asked to contribute a special menu to the book she was writing at the time on the new breed of American chefs. He responded with a spring dinner that included this artichoke recipe.

This dish was a result of what I think of as Bill's transition phase, circa 1984. By the next year, Craig Claiborne quoted Bill in the *New York Times*: "I try to avoid present-day California style of cooking. I would never put goat cheese in a traditional Southern dish!"

This recipe is not a traditional Southern dish, but in spite of his own disclaimer I think this is an excellent example of Bill's cooking aesthetic, which—not unlike "California style"—was fresh, simple, and succinctly flavored.

Serves 4

4 large artichokes
1 T. olive oil
1 t. lemon juice
6 oz. goat cheese
1 egg
1 clove garlic, minced
1 T. chopped basil
1 t. chopped rosemary
1 T. bread crumbs
salt and pepper to taste
olive oil
white wine
mustard vinaigrette (such as La Résidence house vinaigrette, page 36)

Trim the artichokes, removing the outer leaves, cut off the stems, and scoop out the chokes. Cook in a large pot of boiling salted water, seasoned with 1 T. oil and 1 t. lemon juice until tender, about 30 minutes or so.

Mix together the cheese, oil, egg, garlic, basil, rosemary, bread crumbs, salt and pepper. Divide the mixture into 4 portions and spoon in the center of the artichokes.

Place the artichokes in a deep pan and drizzle with olive oil and enough white wine to cover the bottom of the pan. Cover and bake in a 375° oven for 25 minutes or until the cheese mixture is just set.

Uncover and chill. Open the artichokes up like flowers to serve and surround with mustard vinaigrette. Drizzle a little sauce on the leaves as well.

Crab Soup

"She crab soup," a Charleston specialty, is characterized by the addition of crab roe, which gives richness to the soup. Because crab roe deteriorates so quickly and is impossible to find in most inland fish markets, Bill served his version garnished with chicken eggs, the yolks hard boiled and sieved, and minced scallion tops.

Serves 8 to 10

1/2 c. celery, finely chopped
1 c. scallions, white part only, finely chopped
6 T. butter
6 T. flour
2 1/2 c. milk
2 1/2 c. shrimp or chicken stock
1/4 t. nutmeg
1/4 t. white pepper
1/4 t. cayenne (or less)
1 lb. picked backfin crabmeat
4 c. heavy cream
3 T. (or more to taste) sherry, preferably Amontillado
salt to taste

finely chopped scallion tops
3 hard-boiled egg yolks, mashed through a fine sieve

Sauté the celery and scallions in butter until soft. Add the flour and cook for about 4 minutes, or until the mixture thickens. In a separate pan, heat the stock and milk together almost to the boiling point. Pour the hot liquid into the flour mixture, stirring to incorporate. Simmer while stirring for 5 minutes longer. Stir in the seasonings, crab, cream, and sherry.

To serve, reheat just until the soup steams. Garnish with chopped scallions and sieved hard-boiled egg yolks.

Garlic Soup with Mushrooms

Bill introduced this soup as a starter for a menu featured in *Redbook* magazine. The recipe evolved from the classic garlic and bread soup of Southern France, which we offered at La Résidence. This version was served at Crook's when Bill's cooking style was still decidedly French.

Serves 6 to 8

1 medium onion, coarsely chopped
2 T. butter
12 large cloves garlic, peeled
6 c. chicken stock
6 slices stale French bread
salt and pepper
1 c. heavy cream (or less)
1 1/4 c. thinly sliced mushrooms
chopped fresh herbs such as parsley, chervil, and chives

In a large saucepan or Dutch oven, sauté the onions in butter until translucent. Add the whole garlic cloves and sauté for 2 more minutes. Add the stock and stale bread and simmer 20 to 30 minutes until the garlic cloves are tender. Purée the mixture in a food processor or blender until smooth. Strain through a large sieve. Season with salt and pepper. Thin to desired consistency with the cream.

While the stock mixture simmers, sauté the mushrooms in butter until tender. Stir into the soup base and serve with a garnish of fresh herbs.

Marmite Provençale

This soup sounds like it's been misplaced here, but I found it in Bill's handwriting filed with his early Crook's recipes. A note at the end said, "$8.95 with salad. It will sell."

Serves 6 to 8

2 T. olive oil
2 bulbs fennel, chopped
4 leeks, chopped
2 garlic cloves, chopped
1/2 c. vermouth
4 c. fish stock or clam juice
1 14-oz. can diced tomatoes
pinch of saffron
one long strip of orange zest
1 lb. mixed uncooked seafood (e.g., peeled shrimp, scallops, firm-bodied white fish)
1 c. cream
4 T. cornstarch dissolved into 6 T. cold water

In a Dutch oven, sauté the fennel and leeks in the oil over medium heat for 3 to 4 minutes. Add the garlic and sauté until tender, but not golden. Add the vermouth, fish stock, tomatoes, saffron, and orange zest. Simmer for 25 minutes. Remove the zest.

Add the seafood and cook for 3 to 5 minutes. Stir in the cream and cornstarch mixture. Simmer for a few minutes longer until the soup thickens slightly.

Mediterranean Vegetable Soup

This hearty soup, a variation of Provence's *soupe au pistou*, was a staple on the early Crook's menu.

Serves 10 to 12

1 lb. white beans (any kind)
8 c. water
1 onion, peeled and quartered
1 T. salt
2 cloves garlic, peeled and sliced in halves
red pepper flakes
1 sprig fresh thyme
white ends of 2 medium leeks, chopped
1 large onion, chopped
1 clove garlic, minced
2 stalks celery, chopped
3 carrots, chopped
1 bulb fennel, chopped
6 c. chicken stock
1 14-oz. can diced tomatoes or 3 fresh chopped, peeled, and seeded tomatoes
1 t. grated orange zest
1/4 t. saffron
2 t. fresh thyme leaves, chopped
salt and pepper
large croutons (page 31)
Parmesan cheese

Cover the beans in water and soak overnight. Drain.

Add the quartered onion, salt, halved garlic cloves, red pepper flakes, and thyme. Simmer until the beans are tender but not mushy, about 2 hours.

Drain the beans and set aside to cool a bit.

Meanwhile, sauté the chopped leeks, onion, garlic, celery, carrot, and fennel. Add the beans, chicken stock, tomatoes, and remaining seasonings. Simmer for 20 minutes. Add a little water or stock if the soup becomes too thick.

Taste and adjust the seasonings.

Serve the soup hot, garnishing each bowl with a large crouton sprinkled with grated fresh Parmesan cheese.

Oriental Mushroom Soup

Like many of the soups served at Crook's in the early days, this light soup is obviously not a bit Southern. I've left the recipe exactly as I found it on Bill's note card (not a single measurement!) in homage to one of his mentors, Elizabeth David. He revered her cookbooks, and the two of them struck up a correspondence after Bill referred to her in one of his articles. "Oh, what nice understanding and sensitive things you have written about my *Italian Food*," she wrote him. "In America, nobody buys it, and I can understand why. No cups or spoons."

Boil strong chicken stock (reduce well). Add a little soy sauce—be careful, it's salty—a little Tabasco and sherry to taste (a good bit). Add thinly sliced oyster mushrooms. Boil until tender (about 10 minutes). Taste again for sherry and soy sauce. Garnish: Heat soup. Add sliced scallions, trimmed enoki [mushrooms].

White Bean Soup

Most American bean soups are simple and a bit bland, most of the flavoring stemming from ham hock. Senate bean soup, served daily for the past hundred years on Capitol Hill, is a perfect example, using just the most basic ingredients—beans, ham hock, onions, salt and pepper, and water.

This soup doesn't pretend to be Southern. It is Tuscan in style, containing no pork at all, and is more heavily seasoned than our grandmothers' bean soups.

Serves 8 to 10

1 lb. dried white beans
4 T. olive oil (or more if needed)

2 carrots, peeled and chopped

2 stalks celery, chopped

1 medium onion, chopped

1/2 small cabbage, chopped

1/2 green pepper, chopped

1 head fresh garlic (about 10 cloves), cloves separated and peeled, but not chopped

6 c. or more chicken stock (enough to cover the beans)

1 14-oz. can tomatoes

2 t. dried thyme

1 1/2 t. ground cumin

1 t. red pepper flakes

salt and pepper

diced pancetta or bacon

1/2 c. fresh basil, chopped just before serving

Soak the beans in water overnight. Drain.

In a Dutch oven, sauté the carrots, celery, onion, cabbage, green pepper, and garlic in olive oil until the vegetables are soft. Add the softened beans and pour in chicken stock to cover the vegetables plus an extra inch. Add the tomatoes and seasonings. Cover the pot and simmer the soup, stirring occasionally for 2 hours. If the soup becomes too thick, add more stock or water and adjust the seasonings. Serve warm, sprinkled with diced pancetta or bacon.

In warm weather Crook's served this cold, puréed until completely smooth, then garnished with chopped basil.

BREADS

Black Pepper Cornbread

There's no better accompaniment to collards or hoppin' John than this quick bread. Crook's still uses this recipe, as does Bill's former protégé Robert Stehling at Charleston's Hominy Grill.

Makes 8 wedges

1/2 c. flour
2 T. sugar
3/8 t. baking soda
1 T. baking powder
1/4 t. salt
1 c. plus 2 T. cornmeal
1 3/4 c. buttermilk
2 1/2 T. butter, melted
1 large egg
1/4 t. fresh cracked black peppercorns

Preheat oven to 450°. Butter a 9 x 2-inch round cake pan and coat the inside with 2 T. cornmeal. Sift the flour, sugar, baking soda, baking powder, and salt into a mixing bowl. Sift in 1 c. of cornmeal.

Beat the buttermilk and egg together with the melted butter.

Fold the dry flour mixture with the liquid mixture, using a few quick strokes, being careful not to overmix. Pour the mixture into the prepared pan. Sprinkle with cracked black peppercorns. Bake for 30 minutes until golden brown and the bread is pulling away from the sides of the pan.

At home Bill would add 1 c. grated cheddar cheese and 2 T. chopped fresh jalapeño peppers to this recipe when he served it with his family chili (page 185).

Jalapeño Hushpuppies

Makes about 36 hushpuppies

2 c. yellow cornmeal
1 1/4 t. salt
1 c. buttermilk
2 eggs
1/4 c. melted shortening
2 T. finely chopped scallions

1 1/2 c. grated cheddar cheese
4 T. seeded, chopped jalapeño peppers
fat for deep frying: shortening, lard, vegetable oil, or a combination

Sift together the cornmeal and the salt. Beat the buttermilk and eggs together. Add to the cornmeal mixture and beat well. Stir in melted shortening. Stir in the scallions, jalapeños, and grated cheddar cheese. Let stand at room temperature for about 15 minutes.

Heat the deep-frying fat to 365°. Cook a test hushpuppy by dropping a tablespoon-sized ball of the batter into the hot fat. Cook for about 2 minutes or until it rises to the surface and has browned. Remove from the fat and slice in half. If the hushpuppy is not cooked through, add a little more cornmeal to the batter. If the outside is very rough and the inside is too heavy, add a little buttermilk.

Proceed, cooking the puppies about 2 to 3 minutes until golden brown.

CONDIMENTS AND SAUCES

Crook's Corner Cajun Salt

By the end of the 1980s, two clear cooking styles were gaining popularity around the country: low fat and fast. For the first time, Bill was not on the cutting edge of a trend. At home he loved nothing more than creating a meal from scratch. Even chicken stock could be found routinely simmering in his Carrboro kitchen. Like most truly good cooks, he found joy not only in the eating but also in the process of creating a fine meal.

However, Bill was well aware that most folks don't have the time or inclination to spend hours in food preparation. Sensing that New Orleans chef Paul Prudhomme was on to something, Bill concocted Crook's Corner Creole Mustard and Crook's Corner Cajun Salt for mass production. These seasoning mixtures were introduced to gourmet stores around the South in the early 1990s in packages that included quick, low-fat recipes. The salt and mustard are no longer available commercially, but both recipes are well worth the effort to make and keep on hand at home.

1 T. salt
1 1/2 t. ground cumin
2 t. red pepper flakes
1 1/2 t. dry mustard
1 1/2 t. crushed fennel seed
1 1/2 T. black pepper
2 T. paprika
1/4 t. allspice

Stir all of the ingredients together until well blended. The seasoning will keep in an airtight container for several months.

Crook's Corner Creole Mustard

Like Bill's Cajun salt, this mustard mix is no longer available in stores, but it is simple to make and provides a terrific base for several recipes in this collection, including mustard lover's steak (page 139), salmon with pebbly mustard sauce (page 129), and green and gold dressing (page 117). On the product label Bill said of this mix: "The mustard lover's mustard, hot as a Louisiana summer, and pebbly with whole mustard seeds."

Makes about 2 c.

1/4 t. celery seed
1 1/4 t. salt
1 t. sugar
8 T. whole mustard seed
6 T. ground mustard

Mix together all of the ingredients. Store in airtight container for up to 6 months.

Curry Spice Mix

For chicken country captain (page 133) and other curries.

Makes about 1/3 c.

1/2 t. whole cloves
1 t. cardamom seeds
6 t. coriander seeds, lightly toasted
4 t. cumin seeds
4 t. powdered turmeric
black and cayenne pepper (optional)

Grind the seeds together in a spice grinder. Stir in the turmeric. For a hotter curry, add peppers to taste.

Blue Cheese Dressing

This thick dressing is similar to the house dressing served at the Country Squire Restaurant where Bill first worked as a waiter, or that of Durham's sorely missed Hartman's Steakhouse, another of our former college haunts.

Makes about 3 c.

1 c. buttermilk
1 1/2 c. Crook's house mayonnaise (page 119)
1/2 t. black pepper
1/8 t. salt
1/2 t. thyme
1 t. dill weed
1 c. crumbled blue cheese

Whisk together. Stir thoroughly before serving on salad greens of your choice.

Crook's House Dressing

What a departure from the house vinaigrette that we used on *salade verte* at La Res! The tomatoes should be ripe from the local market, which means that this is a summertime item.

Makes about 6 c.

2 c. chopped tomatoes, blanched, peeled, and seeded
2 c. chopped scallions
zest and juice of 1/2 orange
1 t. basil
1/4 t. black pepper
1/2 t. salt
1/2 t. sugar
1/4 t. celery seed
1/3 c. apple cider vinegar
1 1/4 c. peanut oil
1 T. Grey Poupon mustard

Combine all of the ingredients and serve over mixed greens.

Green and Gold Dressing

"Green from fresh herbs and gold from the mustard seeds, this dressing is great with watercress or endive, and makes a piquant, light sauce for grilled shrimp or a rare London Broil." That was Bill's description of this dressing on the package of Crook's Corner Creole Mustard.

Makes about 1 c.

1 T. Crook's Corner Creole Mustard (page 115)
2 T. vinegar
1/8 t. salt
1 t. minced scallion
3 T. chopped fresh herbs (basil, parsley, tarragon, chervil, chives, and mint)

1/4 ripe avocado
1 T. cream
1/2 c. salad oil

Combine all of the ingredients except the oil in a processor or blender. Blend for 1 minute, then add the oil slowly in a steady stream while the machine is running. Let stand 30 minutes before using. Will keep a day or two in the refrigerator.

Herb Vinaigrette

Makes 1 1/4 c.

1/4 c. Dijon mustard
1/4 c. water
2 T. white wine vinegar
1/2 c. olive oil
1 T. each chopped parsley, chives, chervil
salt and pepper to taste

In a metal mixing bowl, warm the mustard, water, and vinegar over a burner. Off the heat, slowly add the olive oil. Cool and add fresh herbs and seasonings to taste.

Yogurt Basil Vinaigrette

Makes about 4 c.

2 c. yogurt
1 c. Crook's house mayonnaise (page 119)
1 clove pressed garlic
1 large cucumber, peeled, seeded, and diced
2 T. finely diced scallions
2 t. curry powder
1 1/2 T. dried basil

1/2 t. salt
1/2 t. black pepper
1/2 t. ground celery seed

Mix together all of the ingredients and serve chilled over cold salmon, tuna, shrimp, or scallops.

Crook's House Mayonnaise

Used on sandwiches and as a base for tartar sauce (page 120) and other salad dressings.

Makes about 3 c.

4 egg yolks
1 t. dry mustard
1 t. salt
4 T. cider vinegar
2 1/2 c. peanut oil

Blend the egg yolks, mustard, salt, and vinegar in the processor for 30 seconds. While the processor is still running, slowly add the oil—in very thin streams at first, then more quickly toward the end until the mixture turns light and thickens. Store in the refrigerator.

Cocktail Sauce

Besides tartar, this is the other sauce served with Gene Hamer's favorite seafood platter fried "Calabash style" at Crook's. Calabash, a tiny coastal village with almost as many restaurants as citizens, is considered by North Carolinians to be the seafood-eating capital of the Atlantic.

Makes 2 c.

1 c. bottled chili sauce (such as Heinz)
1/3 c. bottled ketchup
1/3 c. prepared grated horseradish

2 T. water
1 t. lemon juice
1/8 t. black pepper

Mix together all of the ingredients. Serve chilled.

Tartar Sauce

In the early days at Crook's, an exception to Bill's French-influenced menu was a Calabash-style fried seafood platter. This recipe is closer to the New Orleans version of ravigote sauce than conventional tartar sauce. Subtract half of the pickles, add a few T. of ketchup and you have one version of ré-moulade. Either sauce makes a delicious binder for crab or shrimp salads.

Makes 3 c.

2 c. mayonnaise
2 T. chopped capers
2 T. chopped parsley
2 T. finely chopped scallions
4 T. chopped dill pickle
2 t. Dijon mustard
1/2 t. dry mustard
1 T. lemon juice
2 drops Tabasco sauce

Mix together and serve with fried fish or boiled shrimp.

Crook's Tomato Sauce

This is an all-purpose sauce for "wonderful meatballs" (page 135) or for pasta. This recipe probably makes more than you will need for a meal unless you have a very large Italian family! Freeze the leftover sauce for a future meal.

Makes 6 to 8 c.

3 T. olive oil
2 stalks celery, chopped
2 carrots, peeled and chopped
1 large onion, peeled and chopped
1 T. dried basil
1 T. dried thyme
1 clove garlic, minced
1/2 t. salt
1/2 t. black pepper
2 t. sugar
3 28-oz. cans plum tomatoes, with liquid

Sauté the celery, carrots, and onions until soft. Add the basil, thyme, garlic, salt, pepper, sugar, and tomatoes with liquid. Simmer over very low heat for 1 hour, stirring occasionally and adding water to thin when necessary. Purée. Reheat before serving.

SIDE DISHES

Cheese Grits

This side dish shouldn't be limited to its supporting role in shrimp and grits. Serve it with ham or bacon and eggs for a hearty breakfast.

Serves 4

1 c. stone-ground or quick grits (not instant)
4 c. water (or milk for creamier grits)
1 c. cheddar cheese
1/4 c. Parmesan cheese
4 T. butter
1/2 t. salt
1/8 t. white pepper

pinch of cayenne pepper
1/4 t. Tabasco sauce

Cook the grits according to package instructions for 1 c. dry grits. Turn off the heat and add the remaining ingredients to the sauce pan. Stir until just mixed and serve immediately.

Dirty Rice

Because Bill loved innards, he often made dirty rice, a Southern Louisiana dish. Down in Cajun country this is a meal in itself, but Cajuns also serve it as a side dish accompanying fried chicken.

Serves 4 to 6

about 3 1/2 c. water
8 oz. mixed chicken livers and gizzards
1 medium onion, chopped
1/2 c. chopped celery
1 clove garlic, pressed
3 T. butter
1 c. raw white rice

Blanch the livers in lightly salted boiling water (about 3 1/2 c.) just until firm. In the same water, simmer the gizzards until cooked through. Remove the meat and cut into small dice. Reserve the cooking liquid.

Sauté the onions and celery in butter. Add a little pressed garlic. Stir the raw rice into the mixture. Add 2 1/4 c. of the leftover cooking stock. Cover the pan and cook over low heat for 15 minutes or until rice is soft.

Hoppin' John

I asked John Currence, now chef and owner of City Grocery in Oxford, Mississippi, what his favorite dish was while he was working at Crook's. "Hoppin' John!" he answered without a moment's hesitation. John recalls sitting in the walk-in cooler at Crook's gulping down big spoonfuls of this dish cold, straight from its gallon storage container.

An old Gullah combination of ingredients grown in the Carolina Low-country, hoppin' John is traditionally served on New Year's Day along with collards for good luck. You can have good luck any day of the year at Crook's. This dish is perpetually on the menu.

Serves 3 to 4

2 c. cooked black-eyed peas
2 c. cooked rice
1 c. chopped fresh tomato
1/2 c. chopped scallions
1/2 t. salt
1/4 t. black pepper
grated cheddar cheese

Heat the rice and peas separately if they're cold. (Add 3 T. water to the rice, cover, and steam briefly) In a sauté pan, combine the rice and peas lightly, sprinkle with chopped tomato and scallions seasoned with salt and pepper. Cover and heat just until warm. Serve topped with grated cheese.

Curried Peaches

Bill was born and raised on the border between North and South Carolina. Whenever the subject of barbecue was broached, he claimed North Carolina as home; when referring to shrimp and grits, he became deeply South Carolinian. In the case of peaches, his south-of-the-border persona emerged. Anyone traveling through Gaffney on I-85 has gawked at the huge, peach-shaped water tower there surrounded by peach orchards and ramshackle fruit stands. This is Bill Neal country—he grew up just up the road from that startling monument.

Next time peach season rolls around try this simple recipe, a variation of the curried fruit served commonly at Southern brunch parties along with cheese grits and ham.

Serves 4

4 freestone peaches
4 T. softened butter
4 T. light brown sugar
1/2 t. mild curry powder

Peel the peaches by plunging them for a few seconds into boiling water, then immediately into ice water. The peel should be easy to slip off.

Split the peaches, discard the pits, and place the halves cut-side up in a lightly buttered baking dish. Put a small dab of butter in each cavity. Mix together the sugar and curry powder and sprinkle on top of the peaches.

Broil the peaches on the lower rack of the oven under high heat until bubbling, about 6 to 8 minutes. Serve warm.

Stuffed Sweet Potatoes

This side dish is sometimes part of Crook's vegetable medley, usually served next to wilted spinach and scalloped tomatoes.

Serves 4

2 average-sized sweet potatoes, baked until tender
2 T. raw honey
1 ripe, medium peach or pear, peeled and chopped
1 egg yolk, beaten lightly with a fork
2 T. melted butter
salt to taste
pinch of cayenne
pinch of cinnamon
1 egg white

Cut the baked potatoes in half and carefully scoop the insides out of their skins, leaving the skins intact. Mash the potatoes.

Mix together the potatoes with the remaining ingredients except the egg whites (the mixture should be a little lumpy).

Whip the egg white with pinch of salt. Fold into the potatoes.

Stuff the potato skins or use individual ramekins if you prefer.
Bake in a 400° oven for 15 minutes or until puffy.

Whipped Potatoes

Served with Cajun steak (page 138) and other beef dishes at Crook's.

Serves 6 to 8

3 lbs. russet potatoes
1 stick (1/2 c.) melted butter
1/4 t. ground white pepper
1/4 t. freshly grated nutmeg
1 t. salt
1/2 c. half-and-half

Peel the potatoes, chop coarsely, and boil in salted water until soft. Drain.
Place with the remaining ingredients in a mixing bowl and beat until fluffy.
Serve warm.

Red Slaw

On my first visit to Bill's family's home in the country, I was taken to the
family's favorite dining spot, Red Bridges Barbecue in nearby Shelby, for
chopped pork barbecue, hushpuppies, and an odd, sweet, marinated cabbage concoction these folks called coleslaw. This side dish, very different
from the tangy mayonnaise-based slaw I grew up eating in South Mississippi, was an acquired taste for me. Now I hardly enjoy barbecue without it.

Here is Bill's version of Red Bridges slaw, served at Crook's. This type of
coleslaw is served routinely in the Piedmont area of North Carolina but is
found almost nowhere else.

Serves 8 to 10

1 small head cabbage
1 14 1/2-oz. can tomatoes, diced

1/2 green bell pepper, chopped
1 3-oz. jar pimientos, drained and chopped
1/2 c. cider vinegar
1/4 c. sugar
1/2 T. hot sauce
3/4 t. salt
1/8 t. black pepper

Chop the cabbage finely. In a blender or food processor, combine the tomatoes, bell pepper, and pimientos. Process for a few seconds until the vegetables are chopped finely, but are not mushy. Mix together in a bowl the cabbage, the tomato mixture, and the remaining ingredients. Chill at least 1/2 hour before serving.

MAIN COURSES

Catfish in Creole Sauce

Bill contributed this recipe to a book called *New American Chefs and Their Recipes* (1984), by Lou Seibert Pappas. Clearly Crook's Southern identity had not yet jelled in 1984 when the book was published. The chapter on Bill featured garlic soup with mushrooms, artichokes baked with goat cheese, fish in Creole sauce, and fresh fruit plate.

The original recipe called for swordfish, but now that fresh catfish is readily available and is arguably the most Southern of all fish, Crook's usually serves it this way.

Serves 4

4 catfish fillets
3 bell peppers—1 green, 1 red, 1 yellow—cut into thin slivers
1 medium onion, sliced into slivers
2 cloves garlic, minced
1/4 c. finely diced ham
3 T. bacon grease or vegetable oil

1 c. okra, sliced thinly into rings
2 ripe tomatoes, diced
fresh basil
4–8 drops Tabasco sauce
salt and pepper

Arrange the fish fillets on a greased baking sheet. Preheat the oven broiler.

Prepare the sauce by sautéing the peppers and onions in 2 T. bacon grease or oil for about 5 minutes, until soft. Add the garlic, continue cooking for 2 minutes more, and then add the ham.

Begin broiling the fish.

In a separate pan, sauté the okra in the remaining tablespoon of grease or oil for a couple of minutes. Add the tomatoes, seasonings, then the peppers and onions. Heat for 1 minute while the fish finishes cooking. Serve the fillets on a platter covered with the vegetable mixture.

Mussels Marinière

Another vestige of Crook's pre-Southern era—a classic recipe for mussel lovers.

Serves 6 to 8

4 T. butter or olive oil
6 cloves garlic, chopped coarsely
3 c. chopped onions
grated zest and juice of 3 lemons
2 c. dry vermouth
1 bottle dry white wine
2 c. fish stock or clam juice
2 T. chopped fresh thyme
2 T. dried thyme
2 T. basil
4 bay leaves
1/2 t. black pepper
1/2 t. red pepper flakes

4–5 dozen fresh mussels, rinsed and cleaned
about 4 T. extra butter
chopped scallions including the green part
chopped fresh parsley

Sauté the onions and garlic in oil until soft. Add the lemon juice and zest, vermouth, wine, stock, and seasonings. Simmer for 20 minutes.

Before serving, reheat the broth until it simmers. Check the mussels to see if any have opened. If so, discard. Add the closed mussels and cook a few minutes until the shells open. Serve in large bowls with a spoonful of butter added to each one, then garnished with scallions and parsley.

Broiled Oysters

Crook's offered these oysters as a main course, but the dish also makes a lovely appetizer.

Serves 4 as a main course

4 T. butter
2 c. sliced scallions
1/2 c. minced celery
2 large cloves garlic, minced
1 t. dried tarragon
Tabasco sauce to taste
2 dozen oysters
bread crumb topping (recipe follows)
buttered rice

In a sauté pan, heat the butter and cook the scallions, celery, garlic, and tarragon until the vegetables are tender but not brown. Add a few drops of Tabasco.

In a buttered casserole or individual ramekins, spread the oysters in a layer. Sprinkle the scallion mix on top, followed by the bread crumb topping. Broil until hot and crumbs are brown on top. Serve with buttered rice on the side.

BREAD CRUMB TOPPING

1 c. dry bread crumbs
zest of 1 lemon
2 T. melted butter
salt and pepper to taste

Stir together all of the ingredients, combining well.

Salmon with Pebbly Mustard Sauce

Here is another recipe in which Bill put to use Crook's Corner Creole Mustard. His words on the mustard package insert read: "This sauce is pebbly from the whole mustard seeds. Serve it with roasts or just about any meat. Grilled fish steaks—salmon, tuna, etc.—go great with this sauce. Use an appropriate stock to match. Reserve any pan juices and add to the sauce for extra flavor."

Serves 4

4 salmon steaks, grilled, baked, or poached
2 T. butter
2 T. flour
1 T. Crook's Corner Creole Mustard (p. 115)
1 1/4 c. chicken or fish stock
1/2 c. milk
salt and white pepper to taste
1 T. or more chopped parsley

Melt the butter in a saucepan over low heat. Add the flour and cook as a roux, stirring for 3 minutes or until it thickens, but does not change color. Add the mustard and cook, stirring, for 2 more minutes. Gradually add stock and milk. Cook, stirring until the sauce thickens. Season to taste. Cover and set aside.

Cook the salmon to your liking. Ladle the warm sauce on the cooked fish and sprinkle with parsley to serve.

Maque Choux with Shrimp

During corn season, maque choux is commonly encountered as a side dish in the heart of Cajun country, but it is almost unheard of outside Louisiana, though its ingredients can be found in most Southern gardens and markets. Bill added shrimp to make this corn dish a light summer supper.

Serves 4

4 slices bacon
2 onions, chopped
1 clove garlic, chopped
1 green pepper, chopped
5 ears fresh corn, cut
1 14-oz. can tomatoes, diced
salt and pepper to taste
1 lb. fresh peeled shrimp

Sauté the bacon in a frying pan until crisp. Spread the bacon on paper towels, leaving the bacon fat in the pan. In the hot bacon fat, cook the onions, garlic, and green pepper until soft. Add the corn and tomatoes, plus salt and pepper, and simmer for 30 minutes. Add the shrimp. Simmer just a minute or two until the shrimp turn pink. Serve over rice, sprinkled with the crumbled bacon.

Shrimp and Grits

Bill's most famous recipe is an adaptation of Charleston's "breakfast shrimp." Shrimp and grits was originally (following the "late unpleasantness," as some Charlestonians still refer to the Civil War) just those two ingredients and salt. The combination was pretty much a novelty outside the Lowcountry before it first appeared on Crook's menu in the mid-1980s.

1 recipe cheese grits (page 121)
1 lb. fresh shrimp
6 slices bacon
peanut oil
2 c. sliced white button mushrooms
1 c. minced scallions
1 large clove garlic, peeled and minced
4 t. lemon juice
Tabasco sauce
salt and pepper
2 T. chopped fresh parsley

Prepare the grits and hold in a warm place or on top of a double boiler over simmering water.

Peel the shrimp, rinse, and pat dry.

Dice the bacon and sauté lightly in a skillet until the edges of the bacon are brown, but the bacon is not crisp. Remove from heat and drain on paper towels; then crumble.

Add enough peanut oil to make a layer of fat about 1/8 inch thick. When the oil is quite hot, add the shrimp in an even layer. Turn the shrimp as they color; add the mushrooms and sauté, stirring, for about 4 minutes. Add the scallions and garlic. Heat and stir for about 1 minute more. Then season with lemon juice, a dash or two of Tabasco, salt and pepper to taste, and parsley.

Divide the grits among 4 plates. Spoon the shrimp over, sprinkle with crumbled bacon, and serve immediately.

Trout with Bacon and Scallions

Serves 2

4 bacon slices
5 T. butter
2 8- to 10-oz. whole trout, boned

Bill Neal, sister Jean Marie, Elliott, and Madeline with a Clyde Jones pig, 1988.
Other Jones animal sculptures grace the roof at Crook's.

all-purpose flour
1 c. thinly sliced green onions
2 T. fresh lemon juice
4 t. drained capers
2 t. chopped fresh tarragon
more salt and pepper

Cook the bacon in a large skillet over medium heat until crisp, about 8 minutes. Transfer to paper towels to drain. Crumble the bacon. Pour off all but 3 T. drippings from the skillet. Add 1 T. butter and stir to melt. Sprinkle the fish with salt and pepper and coat both sides with flour, shaking off the excess. Add the fish to the skillet. Cook 2 to 3 minutes. Turn the fish over. Cook until just opaque in the center, about 2 minutes or so. Transfer fish to 2 plates. Pour off drippings from skillet; and wipe skillet clean.

Melt 4 T. butter in the same skillet over medium heat. Add all but 2 T. green onions; sauté 3 minutes. Stir in the bacon, lemon juice, capers, and tarragon. Season the sauce with salt and pepper. Pour the sauce over the fish and sprinkle the remaining green onions on top.

Chicken Country Captain

I grew up eating this delicious adaptation of an East Indian curry, which is enormously popular throughout the coastal Southern states. I don't know a soul who doesn't like it. An excellent party dish, it can be made for a crowd a day ahead of serving. My mother served this at her bridge club luncheons, and we kids couldn't wait to get at the reheated leftovers. Bill fell in love with it in college on a visit to my Mississippi hometown.

Here is the version of country captain Bill served at Crook's. Bill made his own spice mix, a much more aromatic one than the grocery store brand our mother's generation used, though McCormick's Mild Curry Powder is a respectable substitute when perked up with a pinch of freshly crushed cumin seed.

Divide the recipe in half and use one 3- to 4-lb. chicken for 6 portions, but I recommend making it with a large boiling hen (over 6 lbs.) and freezing the leftovers.

Makes at least 12 servings

4 T. bacon fat or butter
3 onions, chopped
3 green peppers, chopped
3 finely chopped cloves garlic
6 c. or more diced poached chicken (2–3 medium-sized chickens or 1 large hen)
2 c. chicken broth (saved from poaching the chicken)
2 28-oz. cans diced tomatoes
2 T. curry spice mix (page 116)
1 t. thyme
1 t. grated orange peel
salt and pepper
Tabasco sauce to taste
1/2 c. currants
toasted almond slivers
chopped parsley or cilantro

Sauté the onions, peppers, and garlic in the fat or butter until just soft. Add the tomatoes, chicken, broth, and all seasonings. Simmer for 30 minutes, adding more broth if needed to keep the stew juicy.

Remove from heat and add the currants. Reheat to serve.

Serve over cooked white or wild rice, or a mixture of both. Sprinkle almonds and parsley or cilantro on top before serving.

Chicken Livers with Mushrooms

I enjoyed this old menu staple at Crook's not long ago and was especially impressed with the delicious rice served with it. When I asked chef Bill Smith the secret, he responded with one word: "Butter." Don't hesitate to add a lot of it to the rice. Bill Neal, fearless when it came to using fat, would have approved.

For 1 serving

6 liver lobes
Pillsbury Shake and Blend Flour
salt and pepper to taste
1/4 t. dried thyme
1/4 t. dried basil
2 T. clarified butter or half butter, half vegetable oil
1 c. sliced mushrooms
2 T. chopped scallions, using both white and green parts
more salt and pepper
1 T. dry sherry
chopped parsley
cooked long-grain rice with lots of butter

Combine the flour, salt and pepper, thyme, and basil. Dredge the livers in the flour mixture.

Sauté the livers in butter for about 5 minutes. Add the mushrooms, scallions, salt and pepper, and sherry. Sauté a few minutes longer until done. Serve over rice with parsley sprinkled on top.

Wonderful Meatballs

These were served at the restaurant with Crook's tomato sauce. This same recipe, baked in a loaf pan, also makes the world's best and juiciest meat loaf. The high proportion of pork in this recipe makes all the difference.

Serves 8

1 lb. ground beef
1 lb. ground pork
2 eggs, beaten with a fork
1 1/2 t. salt
1/2 t. freshly ground black pepper
1 c. bread crumbs
2 t. dried basil

1 t. dried crushed thyme
1 medium onion, chopped
1 stalk celery, chopped
1 green pepper, chopped
1/3 lb. white button mushrooms, chopped
Crook's tomato sauce (page 120)

Mix together all of the ingredients—except the tomato sauce—with your hands until thoroughly blended. Form the meat mixture into balls, about 1 1/2 inches in diameter. Brown in a little olive oil. Add the tomato sauce to the pan and simmer until the meat is cooked through, about 10 minutes. Serve with spaghetti or linguini.

Braised Pork Chops with Baby Limas and Whole Garlic

Who else would combine pork chops, lima beans, and 24 cloves of garlic in one dish? This stew—a little bit Southern, a little bit French, a little bit Italian—is pure Bill Neal. It is fusion cooking in the best sense, a vestige of the garlicky Provence-inspired dishes of La Résidence.

Serves 4

4 thick pork chops
2 T. olive oil
1 large onion, chopped
1/2 c. dry vermouth
1 1/2 c. chicken stock
24 unpeeled cloves garlic (or approximately 1 1/2 heads garlic)
4 short sprigs of fresh thyme
4 short sprigs of fresh rosemary
salt and pepper to taste
1 10-oz. package frozen baby lima beans
2 T. Pillsbury Shake and Blend Flour dissolved in 2 T. cold water
polenta (recipe follows)

Brown the pork in olive oil until golden brown, about 5 minutes on each side. Remove from heat. In the same pan sauté the onion until tender. Add the vermouth and reduce by half. Add the stock, the herbs, and whole garlic cloves. Add salt and pepper to taste. Put the chops in a baking pan or Dutch oven. Pour the sauce over the pork and bake, covered, for 1 hour.

Add 1 package of thawed baby limas to the pan, and stir to distribute evenly. Cook for 20 minutes longer until limas are tender.

To thicken the sauce slightly, add the flour dissolved in cold water and simmer, stirring, for 5 minutes.

Adjust seasonings. Serve with homemade polenta.

POLENTA

4 c. water
1 t. salt
1 c. yellow cornmeal
fresh grated Parmesan cheese to taste

In a heavy pot, bring the salted water to a boil. Add the cornmeal in a thin stream while whisking. Cook over moderate heat, whisking for 2 minutes. Reduce heat to low and simmer polenta, covered, stirring for 1 minute after every 5 minutes of cooking for 45 minutes. Remove from heat and serve warm with grated Parmesan.

Country-Style Roast Ribs

This was one of recipes that Bill developed for the Crook's Corner Cajun Salt label. He wrote on the label, "Country-style ribs in the supermarket are usually cut from the loin, are usually leaner than the usual true spare ribs and are less expensive. They are delicious oven roasted in our barbecue sauce."

Serves 4

2 lbs. country-style pork ribs
4 T. Crook's Corner Cajun Salt (page 114)
4 T. ketchup

2 T. vinegar
2 T. water
2 T. molasses

Rinse the ribs and pat dry. Whisk the rest of the ingredients together until well blended. Spread the sauce on the ribs and let sit at room temperature for 1 hour or more.

To cook, preheat the oven to 325°. Spread the ribs out in a lightly oiled baking dish. Bake for at least 1 hour or until the ribs are very tender.

Cajun Steak

Stimulated by a visit to raucous Lafayette, Louisiana, in the heart of Cajun country, Bill created this dish, one of Crook's most popular entrées.

Serves 4

3 T. salt
2 T. cumin seed
2 1/2 T. red pepper flakes
1 1/2 T. dry mustard
1 1/2 T. fennel seeds
4 T. black peppercorns
6 T. paprika
1 t. allspice
4 cloves fresh garlic
4 rib eyes

In a small food processor, grind together all of the seasoning ingredients. Expect that some of the ingredients, particularly the fennel seed, will grind very coarsely. Rub the seasoning on both sides of the steaks 1/2 hour before pan broiling in a little hot oil on a heavy skillet.

Mustard Lover's Steak

Similar to the French steak au poivre, this is for robust palates and hearty appetites.

Serves 4

2 T. Crook's Corner Creole Mustard (page 115)
2 t. coarse salt
1 t. sugar
1/2 t. coarsely cracked black pepper
1 clove garlic, peeled
1 large sirloin steak, about 2 lbs. and 1 1/2 inches thick

Combine the seasonings in a blender and run until well mixed, or, better, crush by hand in a mortar. Rub the steak all over with the dry marinade and set aside for 30 minutes. Grill to your taste over charcoal. Remove from fire and let sit 5 minutes before slicing thinly against the grain.

DESSERTS

Crook's Hot Fudge Brownies

Despite the variety of wonderful desserts at Crook's, I've never seen my children order anything except this one. To chocoholics, it's absolutely irresistible.

Serves 8 to 10

2/3 c. softened butter
2 c. sugar
4 eggs
4 oz. unsweetened chocolate, melted
1 1/2 c. flour
2 t. baking powder
1/2 t. salt

1 c. chopped pecans
hot fudge sauce (recipe follows)
vanilla ice cream (page 143)

Cream the butter and sugar. Add the eggs, beating just until blended. Add the vanilla and warm, but not hot, melted chocolate. Sift the dry ingredients together and stir in. Add the pecans.

Bake in a greased and floured 9 x 9-inch pan for 25 to 30 minutes at 350°. Cool in the pan to room temperature before slicing into squares.

Top with vanilla ice cream and hot fudge sauce.

HOT FUDGE SAUCE

1 c. heavy cream
1 c. brown sugar
1 c. white sugar
2/3 lb. unsweetened chocolate, cut into small chunks
1 T. butter

In a heavy saucepan stir together the sugars and cream. Cook and stir over medium heat until the sugar dissolves and the mixture comes to a boil. Turn the heat to low and simmer 1 minute. Remove from heat. Add the chocolate and butter. Stir until melted and the sauce is smooth.

Mount Airy Chocolate Soufflé Cake

Bill adapted this chocolate soufflé cake for Crook's from La Résidence's original Kalouga recipe, and some folks believe it's even better.

Serves 12

1 lb. semisweet chocolate
1 c. butter
6 T. brandy
9 eggs, separated
1 c. plus 1/4 c. sugar
1 t. salt

1 t. *cream of tartar*
1 T. *vanilla extract*
lightly sweetened whipped cream

Butter a 9-inch springform pan. Line the bottom with parchment paper. Cut a strip of parchment paper about 30 x 5 inches and line the sides of the pan, forming a collar.

Melt the chocolate and butter in the top of a double boiler. Remove from heat and add brandy.

Beat the egg yolks until fluffy and pale. Gradually beat in 1 c. sugar. Fold into the chocolate mixture. Beat the egg whites with the remaining 1/4 c. sugar, salt, and cream of tartar until stiff peaks form. Fold all together with the vanilla extract.

Pour into the prepared springform pan. Bake in an oven preheated to 350° for 55 minutes, until the center is just set. Let cool on a rack for 20 minutes.

Remove the pan's walls and the paper collar. Continue to cool until the cake reaches room temperature.

Serve with cold whipped cream.

Huguenot Torte

In his *Southern Cooking* Bill wrote about the origin of this dessert. He claimed that it dates from the Huguenot migration of the early eighteenth century, though John Taylor disputes this in his fascinating *Hoppin' John's Lowcountry Cooking*. I hesitated to repeat the recipe until I discovered that several of Bill's former protégés consider Huguenot torte to be the ultimate Crook's Corner dessert, Bill's own favorite. It exemplifies his trademark combination—the use of the best of Southern ingredients with classic French technique.

Serves 8

TORTE

1 1/2 c. *pecans*
2 *eggs*
1 c. *sugar*

1 t. vanilla

1/2 c. flour

2 t. baking powder

1 t. salt

2 medium cooking apples, peeled and chopped finely

Prepare two 9-inch cake pans by greasing the bottoms, lining them with greased and floured wax paper. Preheat oven to 325°.

In a food processor or blender, finely grind the nuts in 2 batches, careful to avoid grinding too long, which will release too much oil.

Beat the eggs in a mixing bowl until doubled in volume. While beating, slowly add the sugar and vanilla and continue beating until the eggs are very thick and light in color. Sift the flour, baking powder, and salt onto the beaten eggs. Sprinkle the ground pecans and apples on top. With a large spatula, gently fold the ingredients together to mix well, but lightly enough to avoid deflating the eggs.

Divide batter evenly between the 2 pans and bake in the middle level of the oven for about 35 minutes or until the sides pull away from the pan.

Place the pans on a rack to cool.

ASSEMBLY

8 pecan halves

cold water

granulated sugar

2/3 c. chilled whipping cream

1 t. sugar

1/2 t. vanilla extract

As the cake is baking, toast the pecan halves lightly. While they are hot, quickly them dip in water, and then roll them in a little granulated sugar until they are lightly coated. Let them dry on the cake rack.

When the cake is room temperature, invert the pan to remove the layers. Peel off the paper, then flip over so that the crusty side is on top.

Whip the cream with the sugar and vanilla extract until stiff peaks form. Place 1 cake layer on a platter. Spread with half the cream. Position the top layer and spread, or pipe with a pastry bag, the remaining cream. Garnish with the sugared pecans. Serve immediately or keep refrigerated until time to serve.

Caramel Ice Cream

Try this with hot fudge sauce (page 140) for a truly sinful dessert.

Serves 6 to 8

1 c. sugar
1/2 c. milk
8 egg yolks
4 1/2 c. cream
1 T. vanilla

Caramelize the sugar by melting it in a heavy-bottomed saucepan over medium heat until it turns a medium amber color. Immediately begin to pour in the milk in a slow, steady stream. Bring the liquid to a boil, stirring to melt the caramel chunks.

Take off the heat while you beat the egg yolks. Pour the hot milk gradually into the beaten egg yolks, whisking constantly. Put the mixture in the pan on low heat, and stir until it thickens and coats a spoon. Immediately remove from the heat and add the cream, which will stop the custard from cooking. Add the vanilla. Cool to room temperature; then refrigerate until cold.

Freeze in an ice cream freezer.

Vanilla Ice Cream

Serves 10 to 12

8 egg yolks
1 1/2 c. sugar
1/2 t. salt
2 2/3 c. milk

3 t. vanilla

5 c. heavy cream

Beat the egg yolks, sugar, and salt together in a large steel bowl. Heat the milk just until it forms a scum on top. Gradually pour the hot milk into the egg mixture. Cook, stirring constantly, over very low heat until it thickens and coats a metal spoon. Do not let the custard come to the boiling point or it will curdle. Immediately stir in vanilla and heavy cream.

Chill and churn in an ice cream maker.

Pear Cranberry Pie

This pie appears on the autumn menu at Crook's and is ideal for Thanksgiving dessert.

Serves 8

6 large or 8 medium pears

2/3 c. fresh cranberries

1 c. sugar

1/2 c. flour (or more)

1 t. cinnamon

1/2 t. ground ginger

1/8 t. salt

juice of 1 small orange (1/4–1/3 c.)

2 t. grated orange rind

1 unbaked 9-inch pie shell

2 T. butter, cut into small pieces

sweetened whipped cream or crème fraiche

Peel the pears and cut them into slices; then halve each slice. Place the pears and cranberries in a large bowl. Mix the dry ingredients together—adding an extra tablespoon of flour if the pears are very juicy. Mix the orange juice and rind into the fruit; then mix in the dry ingredients.

Pour the filling into a pie shell and dot with the butter pieces. Pear sizes vary; so if all the filling won't fit in the shell, discard the excess.

Bake at 425° for 10 minutes. Then turn the oven down to 350° and continue cooking for 45 minutes or more until the pie is almost firm in the middle (the flour causes the filling to set up like a custard).

Serve warm, topped with whipped cream or crème fraiche.

Bourbon Pecan Pie

The ultimate classic Southern dessert, pecan pie is always available at Crook's, served with or without vanilla ice cream.

Makes 2 pies

1/3 c. butter
1 1/3 c. brown sugar
4 eggs
2/3 c. light Karo Syrup
3 c. pecan halves
2 t. bourbon
2/3 t. salt
2 unbaked 9-inch pie shells

Melt the butter and allow to cool to room temperature. Add the sugar, eggs, syrup, pecans, bourbon, and salt, beating until well mixed. Pour into the pie shells.

Bake at 450° for 5 minutes; turn down the oven to 325° and cook another 25 minutes or until the middle of each pie is firm.

Princess Pamela's Buttermilk Pie

Bill discovered Princess Pamela's pie—one of Crook's most popular desserts—at an idiosyncratic soul food restaurant in New York, located in proprietor Pamela's home, a small Harlem apartment. Since the restaurant held only five tables, guests waited in Pamela's living room to be seated.

Gene Hamer recalls, "Bill made himself comfortable on the sofa with his feet propped on the coffee table. When Pamela entered the room, she coolly instructed him to remove his feet by saying, 'This may be homey, but it's not your home.'" Pamela's feistiness made quite an impression on Bill, as did this pie.

Serves 8

1 1/3 c. sugar
1/3 c. butter
2 eggs, separated
3 T. flour
1 1/3 c. buttermilk at room temperature
1 T. lemon juice
1/2 t. nutmeg
1 unbaked 9-inch pie shell

Cream together the butter, sugar, and egg yolks.

Stir in the flour, and then the buttermilk, lemon juice, and nutmeg, mixing well.

Whip the egg whites to soft peaks and fold into the pie batter.

Pour into the unbaked pie shell. Bake for 425° for 5 minutes. Turn the heat down to 325° and continue to bake the pie for 35 minutes or longer until golden brown and set in the middle.

Sweet Potato Pie

Crook's serves this on the fall menu, and my son Matt prepares it every Thanksgiving. The crunchy topping makes this version of a Southern classic extra special.

Serves 8

1 prebaked 9-inch pie shell
1/4 c. cooked, mashed sweet potatoes
4 oz. butter
3/4 c. brown sugar
3 eggs, separated
3/4 c. milk

1/4 t. salt
1/4 t. nutmeg
1/4 t. ground cloves
1/2 t. ground cinnamon
1/4 c. dark rum
topping (instructions follow)

Cream the butter and brown sugar. Then add the sweet potatoes. Beat in the egg yolks and milk, and add the seasonings and rum. Beat the egg whites to stiff peaks. Carefully fold them into the potato mixture. Pour the filling into the pie shell. Make the topping and crumble it evenly on top of the pie.

Bake at 375° for 30 minutes. Reduce the oven temperature to 325° and continue baking for about 20 minutes longer or until the custard is set.

TOPPING

4 T. softened butter
4 T. flour
4 T. brown sugar
4 T. chopped pecans

Stir all of the ingredients together until well mixed.

Bread Pudding

I always thought of this as a New Orleans dessert, more French than Southern. Its main ingredient, crunchy European-style bread made from hard gluten flour, was not available in most Southern groceries outside the Crescent City area until the late 1970s. By that time, well-traveled Southerners had created a demand for baguettes and batards in their own cities.

As in France, New Orleans–style bread pudding was an efficient way to use up the stale bread left over from yesterday's supper. Lately bread pudding has become trendy—I've noticed fancy variations of this humble dessert in elegant dining establishments. The following homey version, though, is easy and inexpensive to make.

Serves 8 to 10

3 large eggs
1 c. sugar
1 t. vanilla extract
3/4 t. ground cinnamon
3/4 t. freshly ground nutmeg
1/2 c. melted butter
1/2 c. raisins and chopped pecans (optional)
1 12-oz. can evaporated milk mixed with 3/4 c. water
4 c. cubed or crumbled stale bread, preferably French style, cubed
bourbon sauce (recipe follows) or sweetened whipped cream

Whisk the eggs until slightly frothy. Add the sugar, flavorings, and cooled butter, and whisk until well blended. Add raisins and nuts at this point if desired. Whisk in milk. Pour bread cubes or crumbs into the egg mixture. Let stand at least 1/2 hour, or until bread is saturated with the liquid.

Pour the pudding mixture into a buttered 2-qt. casserole. Bake at 325° for 45 minutes or until the pudding is puffy and solid.

Serve warm or at room temperature with whipped cream or bourbon sauce—or both!

BOURBON SAUCE

1 stick (1/2 c.) butter
2 egg yolks
1 c. sugar
1/3 c. bourbon

Melt the butter in a heavy-bottomed 2-qt. saucepan. Remove from the heat and let cool. In a mixing bowl, beat the egg yolks lightly, and then gradually whisk in the sugar. Pour the slightly cooled butter slowly into the eggs, and then pour the mixture back into the saucepan.

Place the saucepan over very low heat or in a double boiler, and cook the sauce, stirring constantly, until it thickens. Cooking the sauce too fast or allowing it to boil will result in lumps or curdling.

Stir in the bourbon. Let the sauce cool to room temperature before pouring it over the pudding.

Persimmon Pudding

Persimmon pudding is available at Crook's just for a few weeks in late autumn. Traditionally, the fruit is ready to eat only after the first frost when the wild persimmons have lost their astringency. By then the fruits have fallen off the tree and are turning into mush, the ideal consistency and sweetness for pudding. The trick is to find the persimmons before the birds, squirrels, or other cooks beat you to them.

Bill knew every persimmon tree in town and would scour the streets looking for the mushy ripe fruit to use in this pudding. At Crook's, Bill Smith keeps the tradition alive—he personally knows the persimmon pudding devotees in town, including my husband. We get a call from Smith when the first batch is made every fall, and Drake rushes down to Crook's for his annual persimmon fix.

Serves 16

1/2 c. plus 2 T. butter
1 1/2 c. sugar
3 eggs
2 c. persimmon pulp
1 1/4 c. all-purpose flour
1/2 t. nutmeg
1 t. cinnamon
1/2 t. salt
3/4 c. milk
zest and juice of 1 orange
1/4 c. plus 2–4 T. dark rum
2 T. powdered sugar

Preheat oven to 325°.

Cream the 1/2 c. butter and sugar well. Add the eggs, one by one. Stir in the persimmon pulp.

Sift the flour, spices, and salt together. Add to the butter, alternating with the milk. Stir in the orange zest and juice and 1/4 c. dark rum. Pour into a greased 9 x 12-inch baking dish and bake for about 1 hour, until lightly browned and set in the middle. Remove from the oven to a cooling rack. Let settle for about 10 minutes.

Meanwhile, blend the 2 T. butter, the powdered sugar, and the remaining rum to taste. Prick the top of the pudding well with a fork. Spread the butter-sugar-rum mixture all about to be absorbed by the warm pudding. This is delicious warm, cut into small squares, with a little vanilla ice cream (page 143) to which some bourbon or brandy has been added.

At Home

APPETIZERS AND SOUPS

Corn Chips with Guacamole and Salsa Cruda
Deviled Eggs
Wild Mushroom Sauté
Oysters Rockefeller
Everyday Oyster Stew
Saturday Fish Chowder
Beet and Cucumber Soup
Quick Black Bean Soup
Peanut Carrot Soup
Pumpkin Soup
Vegetable Beef Soup

SIDE DISHES

Cabbage Pudding
East Carolina Coleslaw
Eggplant Fritters
Edwina's Potato Salad

MAIN COURSES

Backyard Spinach Pie
Vidalia Onion Pie

Crab Pie
Creole Gumbo
Elliott's Pasta with Mussels
Pompano Pontchartrain
Shakespeare Sandwiches
Shrimp-Stuffed Mirlitons or Summer Squash
Salade Niçoise
Beef Carbonade
Family Chili
Chicken with Okra
Cajun Broiled Chicken Breasts
Chicken Enchiladas
Groundnut Stew
Cold Roast Chicken with Aioli
Egg Foo Young
Lamb Couscous
Grits and Grillades
Grilled Stuffed Quail
Sausage Chez Vous

DESSERTS AND QUICKBREADS

Biscuits
Fried Pies
Piecrust
Chocolate Chess Pie
French Silk Pie
Villa Teo Pecan Pie

Aunt Lily's Coffee Cake
Date Nut Cake
Pineapple Upside-Down Cake
Vanity Cake
Lemon Cake Pudding
Peaches, Berries, and Dumplings
Blueberry Banana Muffins
Georgia's Gingerbread
Nut Shortbread
Jelly Tarts
Toffee Bars
Bananas Foster
Peanut Brittle

BEVERAGES

Ambrosia
Christian Science Punch
Christmas Parade Hot Chocolate
Sazerac
Shirley Temple
Sidecar

Dad's house was pure fun. Every Saturday he walked with us
to the farmer's market for sweet potato pies. We helped him cook,
or at least tasted things he cooked, for his books. He wrote plays we acted out,
taught us to plant seeds in his garden, invented games for us.
There was never a dull moment.
Madeline Neal

Our food tells us where we came from and who we have become. . . .
One aspect of cooking — and an impetus to it — is the force of hospitality
in the South; here it is a moral obligation of the host to feed the guest.
Bill Neal, Biscuits, Spoonbread, and Sweet Potato Pie

ill had many homes as an adult, but until he was eighteen, home was a house in the country a few miles from Grover, North Carolina, population 400. His father, Frank, worked in town at Minette Mills, but had grown up on his own father's farm down the road, and the Neal kids biked to visit their grandparents, "Mama Neal" and "Daddy Neal," almost every day. Bill's sister Jean Marie recalls, "Everything we did was about food — growing it, harvesting it, cooking and eating it. Our grandparents lived almost completely off their land. Cows, chickens, fruits, vegetables, nuts were all right outside the kitchen door. Even when he was small, Bill was fascinated with the whole process of food preparation and was constantly asking why things were done a certain way." Bill and Jean Marie, the two older children of the family, helped with all the chores. Mama Neal rewarded them with fried pies made from the fruit picked from peach and apple trees in the backyard, and from butter churned from her own cow's milk. Only the flour, White Lily brand, was brought in from the grocery in trade for the eggs Bill and Jean Marie gathered from the chicken house.

Growing up, Bill was an exceptional student and mastered just about everything he attempted. He had a gift for music, playing piano, organ, and trumpet. And he was popular. His tenure as church choir leader "left the place rocking," according to one of the members. Bill's piano teacher recognized Bill's intellectual potential and encouraged him to apply for a full scholarship to Duke University in Durham, just about 200 miles—and yet a whole world—away from Grover.

For the next four years, home was at Duke, first in a West Campus Gothic dormitory, then in a rickety Victorian house on Vickers Street. Bill and I cooked many meals on the house's stove (his first) before graduation in 1971. As jobs were scarce in those days, Bill found a teaching position in North Wilkesboro, North Carolina, where we rented a basement apartment, home for the next year as we settled into married domesticity and discovered the joys of parenthood. We missed the intellectual atmosphere of college life, but found a source of stimulation in *Gourmet* magazine, which transported us vicariously to exotic locales and tantalized us with decidedly un-Southern recipes. The stove replaced the piano as Bill's instrument for entertaining his new audience—students, parents, and teachers from North Wilkesboro High.

In 1973 we moved back to the Triangle area for Bill's graduate studies in English at the University of North Carolina at Chapel Hill. Our Carrboro home was a small apartment near Fitch Lumber Company, the source of materials for all our homemade furniture, including the kitchen table large enough to serve our friends. This same plywood table became the center of our little catering business. On it we decorated wedding cakes, rolled out pie dough, and carved apple birds and radish roses, garnishes for elaborate hors d'oeuvres platters commissioned by the wives of Bill's professors.

The recommendations of these supportive ladies and their friends eventually led to Bill's job as chef at the Villa Teo, and a salary big enough to qualify for a mortgage on a house in a new development south of town called Chatham. We moved our homemade furniture to this "starter home," until our relationship with Chatham's developer R. B. Fitch led us to Jesse Fearrington's dairy farm, later to become Fearrington Village. We sold our house to raise funds to set up our own "mom-and-pop" restaurant in Jesse's farmhouse. Mom, Pop, and little Matt abandoned their brief experiment with suburban life and moved in upstairs.

For the next several years, home and work merged. La Résidence was also our residence, the restaurant kitchen our only kitchen. Our family grew to encompass our cooks, dishwashers, and servers. Since there were no boundaries between home and work, "home cooking" meant experimenting for the restaurant menu, or eating leftovers from the restaurant menu all shared with friends and staff. It was life in a fishbowl, but the quality of food we consumed almost compensated for the lack of privacy. Unlike the domiciles of most young couples with small children, there was not a can of tuna or jar of peanut butter in the house.

Expecting our second child by 1978, we moved to Chapel Hill, seeking what we imagined to be a more normal life. Once again our kitchen was our own, complete with peanut butter. We grew roses in the front yard on Columbia Street, vegetables in the back. On Mondays, when the restaurant was closed, Bill cooked at home with manic energy. He just loved to entertain. A friend recalls, "Bill instinctively knew how to make his guests feel that they were having the best time of their lives, that they could just abandon themselves to pleasure. He made everything look so easy. At home he cooked the simplest things, but everything was perfect."

After at least three more moves following our divorce, Bill finally found his spiritual home, I believe, in a small Carrboro house with a large yard on the corner of Oak and Shelton streets. It was pure mill house on the outside, but the interior was inspired by a magical trip we had taken to San Miguel de Allende in Mexico. Stucco walls and rough quarry tile floors gave the house incongruity, but it had a funky charm, just right for a confirmed nonconformist.

In that house Bill found a freedom of expression that nourished his soul. He immersed himself in landscaping the yard in his own quirky style, inspired by his gardening idol, the *Charlotte Observer* columnist Elizabeth Lawrence. He abandoned vegetable gardening for native Carolina flowers and loved to trade cuttings and seeds with his neighbors. He took great pride in his landscaping and created extraordinary little gardens for our children. Madeline paid him the highest compliment years after his death when she was drawn to a painting of an exquisite garden scene by John Singer Sargent in a London art gallery. "This looks exactly like the secret garden my dad made for me," she exclaimed.

From the Shelton Street house, he could walk to Cliff's Meat Market, Tom

Robinson's fish stand, and his beloved farmer's market to gather ingredients for his culinary experiments. Bill's almost primitive kitchen, the heart of the house, became the laboratory for his cookbooks. Every recipe from *Biscuits, Spoonbread, and Sweet Potato Pie* was tested in his ancient Sears oven. The children and neighbors were always eager to help with the tasting. His friend across the street, Maxine Mills, related, "Once he confided in me, 'I just can't finish the book—too much baking! I just have to give back the royalties.' I said, 'Bill, you have to finish it. You already spent all the money when you took the kids to the Plaza Hotel.' Every day I'd call him and ask what he was going to cook that day, which sort of prodded him along. I helped eat everything he cooked, of course. I'm sure that's why he dedicated the book to me." He never did improve that kitchen, preferring to spend his occasional windfalls on travel and good wine. "I'm sure he spent most of those royalties on Moët et Chandon White Star," Maxine surmised. "He loved it so."

His favorite place to entertain was the large deck outside that kitchen surrounded by old-fashioned roses and a homemade trellis covered with sweet-smelling white clematis. When I think of Bill now, I can see him there serving White Star to neighbors, friends, and family, who enthusiastically sampled his latest recipes, viewed his most recent botanical passions, or watched the children perform plays he wrote for them—all having "the best time of their lives." This scene is, in fact, not much of a stretch of the imagination. Our son Matt and his wife, both great cooks themselves, now live in that house. When I see them cooking a big pot of gumbo in Bill's unchanged kitchen, the center of which is his well-used old chopping block, I experience a slightly eerie but wonderful sort of déjà vu.

In this chapter I have included recipes from all phases of Bill's life. Food from Bill's childhood, New Orleans specialties we tried to re-create early in our marriage, our holiday traditions, the kids' everyday favorites, and some of the best recipes from his magazine articles are represented here. This chapter is all about home cooking—the recipes that I think Bill would want to pass down to his children and their children.

top left: Madeline and Elliott Neal with Amanda and Taylor Bryan at Bill's Carrboro millhouse, 1989.
top right: Bill and Matt Neal, 1982.
bottom: A lesson in biscuit making, 1989. From left to right: Madeline, Bill, and Elliott Neal and Taylor Bryan. (Photograph by Jamie Reynolds, Durham Herald-Sun)

Corn Chips with Guacamole and Salsa Cruda

After a couple of culinarily inspiring visits to Mexico, Bill, true to form, became a connoisseur of guacamole. He wrote in an unpublished article: "The best guacamole is remarkable for its purity. A ripe avocado will be plenty creamy enough and seasonings should all be fresh and ripe. You can add more or less coriander, tomato, jalapeño, to your taste, but avoid sour cream or mayonnaise. Use only Hass avocados, the small ones with rough black skin. When ripe, the flesh should be dense but will give slightly under pressure."

Serves 2 to 4

CORN CHIPS

12 corn tortillas
vegetable oil
salt if desired

Cut each of the tortillas into 6 wedges. Spread on a baking sheet and let dry for 10 or so minutes in a warm place.

Put the oil in a wide skillet to the depth of an inch. Heat to medium high (365° if you have a thermometer). Fry the chips in batches, turning occasionally, until just lightly golden, about 2 minutes in all. Drain and hold in a warm place on paper towels. Repeat until all the chips are fried. Sprinkle with salt if desired.

GUACAMOLE

2 plum tomatoes
1 t. olive oil
1 ripe Hass avocado
1 T. finely chopped jalapeño

1 T. lime juice
4 t. finely chopped red onion
2 t. chopped cilantro
salt to taste

Cut the tomatoes in half from the stem. Sprinkle the halves with olive oil and place on a broiling pan. Broil until soft and a little brown. When cool, scoop out the flesh from the skins. Chop the flesh and reserve.

Remove the avocado from its skin and mash roughly, using a fork. Add the tomatoes and other ingredients.

SALSA CRUDA

Another sauce Bill served with homemade corn chips, this is best, of course, made in the summer with home-grown vegetables.

1 c. finely chopped tomatoes
1/3 c. finely chopped red onion
2/3 c. finely chopped peeled cucumber
1/4 c. finely chopped green bell pepper
1 T. finely chopped jalapeño
1 t. chili powder
1 t. vinegar
1 T. olive oil
salt and black pepper to taste

Mix all of the ingredients and refrigerate for at least 15 minutes before serving.

Deviled Eggs

After he retired from the restaurant and no longer spent Mother's Day cooking for hundreds of other mothers, Bill always made the holiday a festive event for me. With the help of the children, he cooked a grand lunch preceded always by his champagne of choice, Moët et Chandon White Star, uncorked on his Carrboro deck, surrounded at that time of year by the flowers he adored: peonies, irises, and old-fashioned climbing roses.

With the champagne and Shirley Temples for the children, he served pimento cheese with Saltines, tiny ham biscuits, and always these deviled eggs, loved by us all.

Serves 8 to 12

12 large eggs
1/3 c. mayonnaise
4 T. yellow American-style mustard
2 T. India relish, or chopped sweet pickles
salt and pepper to taste

In a large saucepan, bring to a boil enough water to cover the eggs. When the water boils, add the eggs and cook 12 minutes. Immediately rinse in cool water, peel, and slice lengthwise. Remove the yolks and mash with a fork in a small mixing bowl until fairly smooth.

Stir in the mayonnaise and mustard until the mixture is creamy. Add the relish or pickles and season with salt and pepper to taste.

Wild Mushroom Sauté

The first time Bill tried this at home, the mushrooms he used were truly wild, hand-picked by a friend. We loved every bite—and then became violently ill.

Though the detailed instructions and precise measurements of his cookbooks indicate otherwise, this recipe illustrates how Bill really cooked at home—"a little of this, a little of that . . ." I am leaving the recipe as Bill originally noted it.

Use only mushrooms you know to be safe!

slices of stale French bread
clarified butter
girolles, cèpes, or other wild mushrooms, sliced
ham, diced
scallions
garlic
chopped fresh herbs (thyme, flat parsley, a little rosemary, basil)

brandy
heavy cream
salt and pepper
lemon juice

For croutons, sauté 2 slices of stale bread in clarified butter. Remove; put in warm oven.

In butter, sauté sliced mushrooms until barely tender. Add diced ham and sliced scallions. Press in a small amount of garlic. Cook another minute or so. Toss in fresh herbs. Flame with brandy.

Add cream, salt, pepper; boil down a bit. Add a nugget of whole butter. Squeeze in a little lemon juice. Serve over the croutons.

Oysters Rockefeller

Lately I've encountered oysters Rockefeller on several seafood restaurant menus. Apparently this delicacy is having a bit of a revival, though its current form would make Bill roll over in his grave. A bastardized version of the classic is commonly served topped with hollandaise sauce or, even worse, with some sort of gloppy cheese. *Mon Dieu!*

Bill never left the French Quarter in New Orleans without a visit to Antoine's for his fix of oysters Rockefeller. According to local legend, the owner of Antoine's, Jules Alciatore, originally made the dish with escargots until 1899 when a snail shortage forced him to substitute plentiful Gulf of Mexico oysters. The secret recipe for the sauce, said to be so rich it was named after the wealthiest man in America, called for a mixture of greens and absinthe. When Bill tried to re-create it at home, he started with the recipe for a similar version served at another Vieux Carré restaurant, Brennan's.

The secret ingredient, absinthe, now considered almost lethal, was still available in New Orleans back in the 1970s when we first made this recipe. Pernod can be found in most liquor stores today and makes a fine substitute.

Serves 6 to 8

rock salt
1 c. chopped shallots

1/2 c. parsley
1 1/2 c. chopped spinach
1/2 c. flour
1 c. melted butter
1 c. oyster water
2 cloves garlic, minced
1/2 t. salt
1/4 t. cayenne
1/4 c. minced anchovies
4 oz. absinthe (substitute Pernod or Herbsaint)
3 dozen oysters, shucked, and their shells

Fill a pie pan with rock salt for each serving of 6 oysters. Place in oven to pre-heat the salt. While the salt is heating, make the sauce by putting the shallots, parsley, and spinach through a food chopper. Stir the flour into melted butter and cook 5 minutes; do not brown. Blend in the oyster water, garlic, salt, and cayenne. Stir in the chopped greens and anchovies. Simmer, covered, for 20 minutes. Remove cover, stir in absinthe or other liqueur and cook until thickened.

Place the half shells on the hot rock salt. Fill each shell with an oyster. Put the sauce in a pastry bag and cover each oyster. Bake in a 400° preheated oven for about 5 minutes, or until the edges of the oysters begin to curl.

Everyday Oyster Stew

This recipe, more humble than Bill's watercress-laden Southern Cooking version, is closer to the one he usually made at home. The variety of onions in the recipe gives it a nice kick.

Serves 6 to 8

3/4 c. chopped leeks
1/4 c. chopped scallions
1 medium onion, chopped (approximately 1 c.)
3 T. butter
3 T. flour

AT HOME

3 c. milk
3 c. half-and-half
salt and white pepper to taste
pinch of nutmeg
pinch of cayenne
1 t. grated lemon zest
24–30 oysters, shucked
fresh chopped parsley or scallions

Sauté the onions, leeks, and scallions slowly in butter until soft but not brown. Add the flour and cook 2 minutes, stirring. Slowly pour in the milk and cream, stirring constantly. Bring to a boil and simmer 5 minutes. Strain.

Purée the solids and add back to the liquid. Season with salt and pepper, a pinch each of nutmeg and cayenne, and the lemon zest. Add the oysters and simmer another 5 minutes. Serve warm, garnished with chopped parsley or scallions.

Saturday Fish Chowder

Each Saturday, after Bill stocked up on produce at the Carrboro farmers' market, he stopped by Tom Robinson's fish market to survey the weekend's catch. Whatever looked good ended up in this chowder, Saturday's lunch. Use whatever ratio of fish to shellfish you like, 3 to 4 oz. of combined seafood per serving.

Serves 6 to 8

4 carrots, peeled, quartered, and cut in 1 1/2-inch strips
2 leeks, trimmed, quartered, washed, and sliced
4 stalks celery, sliced thinly
1/2 bulb fennel, chopped
1 clove garlic, finely chopped
small pinch of saffron
small pinch of ground clove
2 t. grated orange zest
2 t. dried basil

1 t. dried thyme
1/4 t. red pepper flakes
1 28-oz. can tomatoes, crushed, including liquid
1/2 c. white wine
6 c. chicken stock
salt and pepper to taste
Tabasco sauce to taste
3 boiling potatoes, peeled and chopped into 1-inch pieces
firm-fleshed fish (e.g., monkfish and grouper), cut into large chunks
shellfish (e.g., scallops and peeled shrimp)

In a large Dutch oven, sauté the carrots, leeks, celery, and fennel until almost soft. Add the garlic and continue to cook until the vegetables are soft and translucent, but not browned. Add the remaining ingredients except the potatoes and seafood, and bring to a boil. Simmer for 10 minutes.

When ready to serve the chowder, reheat to a boil, and add the potatoes. Simmer for 5 minutes or more until potatoes soften. Then add the seafood and simmer a few minutes more until the fish is cooked through.

Adjust the seasonings and serve hot.

Beet and Cucumber Soup

Bill was one of the most opinionated men who ever lived. There was nothing lukewarm about him. If I had a dollar for each time I heard him utter, "That was the best [or worst] thing I ever put in my mouth," I'd be a rich woman. In the spirit of Emerson, whose famous line, "Consistency is the hobgoblin of little minds," he loved to quote, Bill had no compunction about reversing his opinions.

Like most Southerners' childhood experience with beets, Bill's was limited to school cafeterias where slimy, overly sweetened slices were served straight from the can. Bill's opinion about beets flip-flopped when in the mid-1970s he tasted borscht in New York's Russian Tea Room. From then on, that humble root's status was elevated from the lowest ranking on the veggie chain to the highest.

Whenever Bill discovered a new taste sensation, he threw himself into learning everything about it, and experimenting with different ways to cook it. I remember having bright red lips after each meal for weeks while Bill went through his beet phase.

Here is one of the concoctions he made during his infatuation with the beet. It's a quicky, using canned beets. Fresh beets, oven roasted before puréeing, are even better.

Serves 6 to 8

2 14-oz. cans beets with juice (not pickled) or 3 c. chopped roasted beets
1 c. peeled, seeded, and chopped cucumber
3 scallions, chopped
3 1/2 c. chicken broth
juice and grated zest of 1 lemon
salt and pepper to taste
sour cream
fresh grated horseradish to taste

Purée the beets with their juice, cucumbers, and the white part of the scallions together until smooth. Add the chicken stock, lemon zest and juice, and salt and pepper. Serve chilled, garnished with sour cream mixed with horseradish, or simply with chopped scallions.

Quick Black Bean Soup

Those who knew him would never expect the word "quick" to be associated with Bill, unless they were referring to his wit. If Bill had lived long enough to see the Slow Food movement emerge from Italy, I'm certain he would have become a zealot.

This soup is an exception to Bill's usual methodical and thorough modus operandi, which would have required hours for softening and simmering dried black beans, not to mention making the stock from scratch. Bill kept these canned ingredients in his pantry for snowy days and other occasions requiring impromptu meals. This soup, topped with grated cheddar, was one of the children's favorites. Bill usually served it with hot cornbread.

2 T. peanut oil
1/2 c. chopped onion
1/2 c. chopped celery
1/2 c. chopped bell pepper
1/2 c. chopped carrots
2 large cloves garlic, chopped
2 t. chili powder
1 t. ground cumin
2 t. paprika
1/4 t. dried thyme
dash of ground cayenne, or to taste
1 14 1/2-oz. can tomatoes, including liquid
2 16-oz. cans undrained black beans
2 c. beef stock
1/4 c. dry sherry or rum
1 T. lime juice

Heat the oil in a large saucepan. Add the onion, celery, pepper, and carrot and sauté until tender, about 7 minutes. Add the garlic and spices and stir for 1 minute over the heat. Add the tomatoes with their liquid, beans, and stock. Simmer slowly for 20 minutes. Purée half the soup in a blender. Then mix the purée back into the rest of the soup. When ready to serve, reheat and add sherry or rum and lime juice. Garnish with grated cheddar cheese or with sour cream and chopped cilantro or scallions.

Peanut Carrot Soup

Bill and his siblings each had a peanut patch at their grandparents' farm. Daddy Neal taught all the Neal children basic gardening skills by showing them how to plant, weed, hoe, and harvest the legumes.

This was one of many peanut recipes Bill and I collected after we married. They were reminders of his childhood and the legacy of his hardworking grandparents.

Serves 8

1 c. onion, chopped
1/2 c. celery, chopped
2 c. carrots, chopped
4 T. butter
2 qts. chicken stock
1 c. smooth peanut butter, preferably Jif
3/4 c. heavy cream
salt and pepper to taste
chopped scallions or cilantro
chopped peanuts

Sauté the onion, celery, and carrots in butter until soft. Add 1 qt. of the chicken stock and simmer for 1/2 hour. Purée in a blender or food processor until smooth. Whisk the peanut butter gradually into the purée. Add the remaining chicken stock, the cream, and salt and pepper. Reheat without boiling.

Serve hot or chilled, garnished with scallions or cilantro and/or chopped peanuts.

Pumpkin Soup

Weekends in North Wilkesboro, where Bill taught high school, were spent scouting the area for appealing restaurants. With the exception of divine fried chicken and home fries from the local Perdue factory's chicken take-out joints, pickings were pretty slim. Whenever possible Bill and I, with baby Matthew in tow, made the hour-long car trip to the best restaurant within reach, Salem Tavern, part of the historic Moravian settlement in Winston-Salem. Back home we tried to replicate many of the tavern's wonderful dishes, including this one. For years we served it at home as the first course of Thanksgiving dinner.

1 large onion, chopped
1/4 c. butter
1 clove garlic, minced
1 T. minced fresh ginger root
1/4 t. ground cardamom
1 t. curry powder
3 c. pumpkin (or butternut squash), peeled, seeded, and cut into chunks
4 c. or more chicken stock
1/2 t. lemon rind
1/2 c. heavy cream
salt and pepper to taste
pinch of nutmeg
crème fraiche or sour cream (optional)

Sauté the onion in the butter until translucent. Add the garlic; sauté for 1 minute more. Add the ginger, spices, pumpkin, chicken broth, and lemon rind. Simmer over low heat for 25 minutes. Remove from heat and purée in a blender or food processor until smooth. If the soup is too thick, thin with a little more stock and adjust the seasonings.

Add the cream before reheating. Season with salt, pepper, and nutmeg. Garnish with sour cream or crème fraiche if desired.

Vegetable Beef Soup

Every family has its favorite vegetable soup, and this was ours. We didn't really measure the ingredients—the idea being to use up the veggies in the refrigerator—but this is pretty close to the norm. I thought this recipe came from my mother, but she disclaimed it. "I would never put chili powder or *beau monde* in my vegetable soup," she protested. Bill or I must have thought her recipe needed a little kick.

Serves 8 to 12

3 lbs. beef shanks
6 c. water
2 c. tomato juice
1 small onion, chopped
1 T. salt
1 T. Worcestershire sauce
1/4 t. chili powder
1/4 t. or more beau monde seasoning
2 bay leaves
1 14-oz. can tomatoes, diced
3 stalks celery, chopped
1 c. fresh or frozen corn
1 c. chopped potatoes
3 carrots, peeled and chopped
1 c. butter beans
1 1/2 c. green beans, cut into 1-inch slices
salt and black pepper to taste

Simmer the first 8 ingredients for 2 1/2 hours in a covered soup pot. Strain the soup and put the liquid back in the pot. Add the vegetables and the salt and pepper. Take the meat off the bone, cut into bite-sized chunks, and add back to the soup. Simmer for another 1/2 hour.

Correct the seasonings, add more water if necessary, and reheat before serving.

SIDE DISHES

Cabbage Pudding

Jim Ferguson teaches an honors course on culinary history at the University of North Carolina at Chapel Hill. His reading list includes Bill Neal's Southern Cooking along with some of the books that Bill admired most, including Brillat-Savarin's The Physiognomy of Taste and Kant's Critique of Judgment. "If it weren't for Bill I wouldn't be teaching this damn course!" Jim told me with a twinkle in his eye. "Bill showed me it was okay to talk about food and think about food—the way food changes, maintains, and reflects culture. He inspired and motivated me to pass on a way of thinking about food with a cultural perspective."

Jim's students love to get together to cook a meal with him every Tuesday. "We still make the old *Southern Cooking* favorites: shrimp and grits, of course, and cabbage pudding, Huguenot torte, wine jelly, herb-crusted pork loin with onion gravy."

Bill's *Southern Cooking* is the only book in which I have ever seen this recipe. He implies that the origin of the dish is the Blue Ridge area, where farmers grow cabbages in vast fields. Whether this dish came from German immigrants who brought cabbage to the New World, or from the Scotch-Irish settlers who later populated most of the Blue Ridge, we don't know.

Bill recommended dressing this up with your favorite tomato sauce if you like.

Serves 4 to 6

2 1/2 qts. water
2 oz. bacon (3–4 slices)
1 dried red pepper pod (or 1 t. dried red pepper flakes)
1 medium-sized head of cabbage (about 2 1/2 lbs.)
3 eggs
1 t. salt
1/4 t. black pepper
1/8 t. cayenne
1/4 t. dry mustard
1 1/2 c. milk or light cream
3/4 c. small cubes of white bread or biscuits
1/2 t. dried thyme flakes
1 T. butter
1/4 c. fine white bread crumbs
2 T. melted butter

In a pot large enough to hold the cabbage, bring the water to a boil. Add the bacon and red pepper. Quarter the cabbage, after removing the dark outer leaves, and add to the pot. Boil for 15 minutes. Reserve the bacon. Refresh the cabbage with cold water and drain well. Remove the core and stem portions of the cabbage and chop roughly. Dab with a paper towel to remove excess moisture.

Beat the eggs with the salt, peppers, and mustard. Beat in the milk and add to the cabbage.

Dice the reserved bacon. Combine with the bread cubes and thyme.

Butter the bottom and sides of a flat-bottomed ceramic baking dish. Sprinkle the bread crumbs over the buttered surface. Pour in the cabbage mixture, even it out, and top with the bacon tossed with the bread cubes and thyme. Drizzle the top with the melted butter. Bake in a preheated 350° oven for 50 minutes, or until the custard is set. Cool for 5 minutes before inverting onto a platter to slice and serve.

East Carolina Coleslaw

Though Bill grew up in that little corner of the world where coleslaw was commonly vinegar-based, he later converted to this more traditional Southern mayonnaise-based salad, just barely sweet. We served it at home as most Southerners do, on hot dogs or with fried or barbecued chicken, ham, or any picnic food.

Serves 4 to 6

4 c. finely chopped cabbage
2 T. freshly grated onion
6 T. mayonnaise
1 t. sugar
2 t. apple cider vinegar
1 t. Dijon mustard
1/4 t. whole celery seed
1/4 t. black pepper
3/4 t. salt

Mix thoroughly all of the ingredients except the cabbage. Then add the cabbage and stir to mix. Chill before serving.

Eggplant Fritters

At the end of the 1980s, Bill was researching recipes for a Southern vegetarian cookbook, a bit of an oxymoron since most Southern veggies are traditionally cooked with one pig part or another. This recipe is one of the best I resurrected from his vegetable file.

Serves 4

1 medium eggplant (about 1 lb.)
1 beaten egg
1 clove garlic
1/4 c. sliced green onions
2 T. fresh chopped parsley
4 T. bread crumbs
1/2 t. salt
1/2 t. baking powder
vegetable oil for frying

Peel the eggplant, cut into 1-inch cubes, and steam over boiling water until quite tender, about 15 minutes. Drain and mash until smooth. Add the rest of the ingredients except the cooking oil. Stir well. Form into small patties and fry in hot oil. Serve immediately.

Edwina's Potato Salad

There are hundreds of variations of potato salad, including mustardy French and warm, bacon-flecked German. Bill grew up eating this version, his mother's recipe, typical of potato salads consumed at church suppers and picnics all over the South.

Serves 6

1 1/2 lbs. new potatoes, peeled and cubed
2 hard-boiled eggs, chopped
1/4 c. finely chopped bell pepper
2 T. finely chopped celery
2 T. finely chopped onion
1/3 c. mayonnaise
2 t. American-style yellow mustard
2 t. sweet pickle relish
1/2 t. salt
1/2 t. black pepper

Place potatoes in a medium-sized saucepan filled with salted water and bring to a boil. Cook about 10 minutes or until tender but not mushy. Drain and cool. Mix together the rest of the ingredients and gently stir them into the potatoes. Chill for an hour or more before serving.

MAIN COURSES

Backyard Spinach Pie

By the time Bill moved to Carrboro, his gardening model was more Elizabeth Lawrence than Daddy Neal. He was such a fan of Miss Lawrence that he edited a compilation of her columns for a book called *Through the Garden Gate*, published in 1987. After that, he devoted his yard to growing flowers and herbs, with one exception. In the bare spots of his perennial borders, the places reserved for summer annuals, he planted spinach when his impatiens and petunias had bloomed out for the season. As soon as the spinach leaves were ready to pick in late fall, he made backyard spinach pie.

Serves 6 to 8

1 unbaked 9-inch piecrust
1 t. Dijon mustard
8 oz. fresh spinach

1 3/4 c. half-and-half
1/4 c. buttermilk or yogurt
4 eggs, lightly beaten
2 T. minced onions
1 t. salt
1/8 t. black pepper
dash of Tabasco sauce
1 1/4 c. grated medium cheddar cheese

Preheat oven to 425°. Paint the bottom of the crust with the mustard and bake 2 minutes. Blanch the spinach in boiling salted water for 2 to 3 minutes. Drain under cold water to stop cooking. Press excess moisture out and chop roughly.

Mix the cream, buttermilk, eggs, onions, salt, pepper, and Tabasco. Layer half the spinach in the piecrust followed by half the cheese; then make a second layer of each. Pour the egg mixture on top of the spinach. Bake at 325° for about 40 minutes, or until set.

Vidalia Onion Pie

This is one of Madeline's favorites from her dad's kitchen.

Serves 6 to 8

3 T. butter
4 small Vidalia onions, or 3/4 lb., enough to equal 3 c. thinly sliced onions
3 whole large eggs
1/2 c. cream
1 c. milk
3/4 t. salt
pinch of cayenne
1 partially baked 9-inch pie shell, lightly brushed with Dijon mustard
1/4 c. crumbled Parmesan cheese
1/4 c. grated Gruyère or other Swiss cheese
1 1/2 t. finely chopped fresh thyme

Preheat oven to 350°.

Melt the butter in a large frying pan and sauté the onions over medium heat until golden brown and all of the liquid has evaporated, about 20 minutes. Remove from heat and cool.

In a small bowl beat the eggs, cream, milk, salt, and cayenne.

Spread the onions in the bottom of the pie shell. Sprinkle with fresh thyme, Parmesan, and Gruyère. Pour the egg mixture over the top. Bake in the top third of a preheated oven for 35 to 40 minutes or until the filling is set and the top is lightly browned.

Crab Pie

Bill would let the children pick out their own live crabs from the barrel at Tom Robinson's Carolina Seafood. Before Bill got down to cooking, preschool-aged Elliott and Madeline would play with the crustaceans, pretending that the crabs were monsters attacking their toy action figures. After the battle, the monsters would meet their cruel fate—as the main ingredient of crab pie. Bill liked to do things the hard way, but I think this is just as good if you let someone else take care of the slaughter and buy lump crabmeat already cooked and picked.

Serves 6 to 8

1 prebaked 9-inch pie shell
1 T. Dijon mustard
6 eggs
1/2 lb. picked lump crabmeat
3/4 c. ricotta cheese
1/3 c. Parmesan cheese
1 c. half-and-half
pinch of nutmeg
1/2 t. salt
1/8 t. black pepper
zest of 1 small lemon
2 T. fresh basil, chopped

Let the pie shell cool, then brush the bottom of it with the Dijon mustard. Beat the eggs lightly; then mix in the rest of the ingredients. Pour into the pie shell and bake at 350° for 50 minutes or until set. Let the pie cool for at least 10 minutes before slicing.

Creole Gumbo

When Bill and I arrived for visits at my mother's house in Mississippi, we were usually greeted with a big pot of gumbo simmering on the kitchen stove. My mother's aunt Ann who lived on the Gulf coast cooked vats of it each year and gave a gallon to each of her nieces and nephews for Christmas. Knowing how much Bill and I loved gumbo, my mother always froze hers, to be thawed out for our homecoming.

Cooking up a pot of gumbo became a ritual for Bill. It meant someone special was coming to visit.

Serves 10 to 12, with leftovers

2 1/2 lbs. shrimp, unpeeled
2 1/2 qts. shrimp stock (recipe follows)
4 T. bacon fat or vegetable oil
6 T. flour
2 medium onions, chopped
1 medium green pepper, chopped
3 celery stalks, chopped
1/2 t. dried red pepper flakes
1 bay leaf
1 t. dried thyme
1/2 t. dried oregano
salt and pepper to taste
3 or 4 links andouille or other smoked pork sausage, sliced (optional)
2 c. okra, tops removed and thinly sliced
Tabasco sauce
5 live blue crabs

1/2 t. gumbo filé (optional)
cooked white rice

Peel the shrimp and make the shrimp stock from the shells. Cover and refrigerate the shrimp until needed.

In a large Dutch oven, make the roux by heating the oil or bacon fat for 2 minutes or so until it is quite hot, but not smoking. With a wooden spoon, stir in the flour. Continue stirring until the flour turns dark (the color of dark brown sugar) but not burned. If the roux develops black spots, discard it and start over.

Add the onions, green pepper, and celery to the roux and sauté for 3 to 5 minutes. Add the red pepper flakes, bay leaf, thyme, oregano, salt, and pepper. Pour in the stock. Add the sausage, if desired. Simmer for 45 minutes. Add the okra and cook for 15 minutes more. Add Tabasco to taste.

Just before serving add the live crabs and, if you like, the gumbo filé. Simmer for 5 minutes. Add the shrimp and simmer just a few minutes longer until they turn pink. Lift the crabs out of the gumbo and cut in half.

To serve, spoon a little cooked rice into each bowl. Add half a crab for each serving. Ladle the gumbo on top.

SHRIMP STOCK

3 qts. water
shells from the peeled shrimp
1 onion, peeled and quartered
1 celery stalk, quartered
2 cloves garlic, peeled and halved
2 t. salt

Place all of the ingredients in a stock pot. Bring to a boil and simmer for a minimum of 20 minutes (the longer you cook the stock, the richer the flavor will be). As the water evaporates, add more to maintain at least 2 1/2 qts. of liquid. Remove from heat and strain the stock to remove solids.

Elliott's Pasta with Mussels

Elliott Neal insisted that I include this recipe, one of his favorite meals at Bill's house when he was nine or ten. He loved to go with his dad to the old (now much lamented) Fowler's Grocery Store on Franklin Street in Chapel Hill to buy "mussels and *Mad* magazines."

Serves 4

4 T. olive oil
2 c. sliced fresh mushrooms
2 cloves garlic, chopped
1 c. sliced scallions
2 t. fresh basil, finely chopped
1 t. fresh thyme, finely chopped
salt and pepper to taste
2 c. diced tomatoes (1 14-oz. can)
1 1/2 c. shucked steamed mussels
1 lb. fettuccini
chopped parsley
lemon wedges

In a large pot, heat water for the pasta.

Heat the oil in a large skillet. Sauté the mushrooms until tender; then add the garlic and scallions. Cook just a few minutes until the scallions become limp. Add the herbs, salt, pepper, and tomatoes. Heat, stirring occasionally, for 10 minutes.

Cook pasta according to package directions. While the pasta is draining, add the mussels to the tomato sauce and cook just until the mussels are hot.

Serve the mussels and sauce over the pasta garnished with parsley and a lemon wedge.

Pompano Pontchartrain

In *French Lessons*, British author Peter Mayle hilariously describes his first French meal, a Gallic refinement of fish and chips. So powerful was Mr. Mayle's experience that he equates it with losing his virginity. I've no doubt Bill would identify with the concept and, with a laugh, reveal that he similarly lost his "gustatory virginity" at a restaurant in New Orleans.

On Bill's first trip to the city, my mother treated us to lunch at Antoine's, New Orleans's oldest and most heralded restaurant, a family haunt for several generations. At her suggestion we ordered pompano Pontchartrain and the ultimate french-fried potatoes, *pommes de terre soufflé*. For nineteen-year-old Bill, the meal was nothing less than an epiphany.

Bill never did replicate that mysterious puffed potato recipe, but years later when pompano became available in the Triangle during its Atlantic season (barely six weeks in the early fall), we made this version of Antoine's incomparable classic pompano Pontchartrain at home and later served it at La Res.

Serves 4

2 T. *canola or vegetable oil*
4 *pompano fillets*
1 c. *butter*
2 c. *lump crabmeat*
lemon juice
salt to taste
lemon wedges

In a heavy sauté pan, cook the fillets in the oil over medium heat, about 3 minutes on each side (depending on the thickness of the fish) or until opaque all the way through. Melt the butter in a small pan. Add the crabmeat just long enough to heat it. Add 1 or 2 drops of lemon juice and salt to taste. Pour the crabmeat and butter over the pompano. Garnish with lemon wedges.

Shakespeare Sandwiches

When I asked Madeline and Elliott about their favorite food at Bill's, they each had a list of their own. One item they both agreed on was this sandwich—memorable not only because they loved the taste, but also because of (or maybe, in spite of) the ritual associated with it. Bill, ever the English teacher, would read aloud from *A Midsummer Night's Dream* or *Romeo and Juliet* while they devoured their sandwiches.

bagels
cream cheese
capers
fresh bean sprouts
sliced fresh tomatoes
salt and pepper to taste
thin slices of smoked salmon

Split and toast the bagels. Spread with cream cheese, sprinkle with a few capers and add the rest of the ingredients.

Shrimp-Stuffed Mirlitons or Summer Squash

Sometimes called "vegetable pears" (not to be confused with alligator pears, a Deep South nickname for avocados), mirlitons aren't seen much in the Carolinas, but they grow almost as prolifically as kudzu in Southern Louisiana. Bill enjoyed this dish in Mississippi, and we re-created it when we returned to Chapel Hill, using eggplant, large yellow squash, or zucchini. Any other kind of summer squash big enough to hold the stuffing will work just fine.

Serves 4 to 8

4 mirlitons (substitute eggplant or summer squash)
1/4 c. butter
1 onion, finely chopped

2 cloves garlic, minced
1 stalk celery, finely chopped
1 lb. fresh raw shrimp, peeled and cut into small pieces
1/2 c. chopped ham
1/4 t. dried thyme
salt and pepper to taste
3 drops Tabasco sauce
1/2 c. grated sharp cheddar cheese
1/2 c. bread crumbs

Cut the mirlitons in half and remove the seeds. Parboil until almost tender. Scoop out the "meat," leaving enough of a shell to hold its shape, and set aside. Melt the butter and sauté the onions, garlic, and celery until tender. Add the raw shrimp and cook until just pink. Mash the mirliton meat and add it to the shrimp mixture. Add the ham. Cook the mixture for about 5 minutes. Add the thyme, salt, pepper, and Tabasco, and mix well. Put the stuffing back into the mirliton shells and top with the cheese and bread crumbs. Bake at 350° until lightly browned, about 20 to 30 minutes.

Salade Niçoise

Like most Americans in the mid-1970s, Bill and I were accustomed to two kinds of tuna dishes: mushy tuna salad and greasy noodle casserole made with canned peas, canned soup, and canned onion rings. We grossly underestimated tuna's appeal until we tried salade Niçoise on our first visit to Southern France. This traditional salad, I've been told, was created to use canned tuna, not the soggy, water-based variety common in grocery stores today, but chunk tuna packed in oil, preferably olive oil, as it is in Mediterranean countries. The dish became popular in the United States by the late 1970s, and then was "improved" when fresh tuna, having become available by the '80s, replaced canned. To Bill this trend was, to use one of his favorite judgments, "gilding the lily."

In the summer, Bill would often serve salade Niçoise (with oil-based canned tuna, always) on his Carrboro deck. Accompanied by a baguette and a bottle of dry rosé, nothing could be better when it's just too hot to cook.

green beans, blanched until tender
boiled new potatoes
oil-packed solid white tuna
Mediterranean-style black olives, such as Niçoise or Kalamata
good ripe tomatoes, cut into wedges
hard boiled eggs, cut into thick wedges
canned flat anchovies
La Résidence house vinaigrette (page 36)
mixed green lettuce

On top of mixed greens, arrange the tuna, beans, potatoes, olives, tomatoes, and hard-boiled eggs. Finely chop a few anchovies and stir them into the dressing. Sprinkle the dressing on top of the salad before serving.

Beef Carbonade

Belgian "beer stew" is not as elegant as its French relatives, such as *boeuf bourguignon*, but more affordable. In graduate school we splurged on this stew, a guilty pleasure, when our vegetarian housemate was away. What did we eat when she was home? A whole lot of potato casserole made with cheese and vermouth. I would have included the recipe in this book, but I don't think I ever want to taste that dish again.

Serves 6 to 8

3 1/4 lbs. beef rump or chuck, cut into 1 1/2-inch cubes
4 T. vegetable oil
2 slices bacon, diced
3 lbs. medium onions, thinly sliced
1 c. beef broth
1 pint dark beer or more
1 bay leaf
1 t. chopped fresh thyme (or 1/2 t. dried thyme)
salt and pepper to taste
3 T. vinegar

6–8 medium potatoes, peeled, boiled, and halved
chopped parsley

In a Dutch oven, brown the beef (in batches) in oil over medium-high heat. Remove from the pan and set aside on a plate. If necessary, pour off excess fat in the pan. Reduce the heat to medium low, add bacon and cook until barely crisp but not too brown. Add onions and sauté until they are soft and golden. Add browned beef, broth, beer, and seasonings. Simmer, covered, 1 1/2 to 2 hours or until meat is tender. If stew becomes too concentrated during the cooking process, add a little broth or water to dilute.

Skim the fat off the surface of the stew and adjust the seasonings. Stir in the vinegar. Cook 10 minutes more. Add the potatoes and heat just until they are warm. Serve garnished with parsley.

Family Chili

During graduate school, Bill and I experimented with every imaginable chili recipe—the more "alarms" the better. After the children were born, we toned down the heat a bit. This is the recipe we always came back to, and the kids still can't get enough of it. Bill served it at his Carrboro home every Christmas Eve with his traditional cornbread recipe, embellished with jalapeño pepper and corn kernels for the occasion.

This recipe makes a relatively thin, soupy chili. If you prefer to eat your chili with a fork, reduce the amount of V8 juice used.

Serves 8

1 1/2 lbs. ground chuck or round
3/4 lb. chuck or round, cut into 1-inch cubes
1 large onion, chopped
1 large green bell pepper, chopped
2–3 stalks celery, chopped
2 large cloves garlic, chopped
1 large can (48 oz.) V8 juice
2 T. chili powder (mild or spicy depending on your company)

1/2 t. cumin
1/4 t. cinnamon
salt and pepper to taste
optional condiments: rice, grated cheddar or queso fresco, sour cream,
chopped cilantro, chopped green onions, Tabasco sauce

Brown all the meat in a little olive oil in a large Dutch oven. Drain excess fat. Add the onion, bell pepper, celery, and garlic, and cook until limp. Add the V8 juice and spices. Simmer, stirring occasionally for 1 hour until the chili thickens. Adjust the seasonings and serve with the condiments of your choice.

Chicken with Okra

Among Bill's recipe cards, most handwritten in his meticulous script, I found this recipe scribbled in a familiar child's hand. I can imagine Bill dictating the recipe as he improvised over the stove, to daughter Madeline, his seven-year-old scribe. This dish is typical of *cuisine du marché* (cooking inspired by the market), Bill's favorite way to cook. Most likely he was drawn to a display of particularly attractive okra at the farmer's market and enlisted Madeline's help to work out a new recipe for Crook's summer menu.

Serves 8 to 12

1 c. vegetable oil
2 chickens, cut into pieces
3/4 c. flour
1 t. curry powder
1/2 t. paprika
1 1/2 t. dry mustard
2 t. salt
1/2 t. white pepper
2 yellow onions, chopped
2 red bell peppers, chopped
1/2 lb. okra, sliced
2 oz. ham, diced

2 cloves garlic, minced
2 14-oz. cans tomatoes, diced
1 c. water
1 1/2 t. salt
1/2 t. thyme

Mix together the flour, curry powder, paprika, mustard, salt, and pepper. Reserve 2 T. of this for later use. Coat the chicken pieces in the flour mixture. Brown the pieces in the oil in a deep, thick skillet.

Remove the pieces from the pan and pour off excess oil, leaving about 2 T.

Add the onions and peppers, sauté for 5 minutes until soft. Then add the okra and garlic. Sauté for another 5 minutes. Sprinkle the reserved 2 T. of the flour mixture on the vegetables and cook until the flour colors slightly. Pour in tomatoes, water, salt, and thyme.

Add chicken pieces back to the pan with the vegetables. Add the ham. Simmer for about 30 minutes or until chicken is done. Correct seasonings and serve.

Cajun Broiled Chicken Breasts

This simple dish, designed for cholesterol-minded home cooks, appeared on the package of Crook's Corner Cajun Salt. I can't say that this was a favorite of Bill's, who never had to watch his weight, but for those of us with slower metabolic rates, it's quite tasty.

Serves 4

4 boneless, skinless chicken breasts
4 t. Crook's Corner Cajun Salt (page 114)
3 t. vegetable oil
1 recipe low-fat Cajun sauce (recipe follows)

Preheat broiler to 450°.

Sprinkle the chicken breasts with the oil and rub in the Cajun salt. Let sit 5 minutes.

Place the chicken on a shallow pan. Cook on the top rack under the broiler for about 10 minutes. Turn and finish cooking about 5 minutes more, being careful not to overcook.

Serve warm with low-fat Cajun sauce.

LOW-FAT CAJUN SAUCE

1 c. yogurt
1 t. Crook's Corner Cajun Salt (page 114)
1/2 c. peeled, grated cucumber
1 clove garlic (optional)

Combine the yogurt, Cajun salt, and cucumber. Add the garlic through a press. Stir well and chill for 10 minutes before using.

Chicken Enchiladas

This is an adaptation of a dish we enjoyed on a trip to San Miguel de Allende, Mexico, in the late seventies. Our hostess's talented Mexican cook was trained in French technique and delighted us at every meal with her hybrid cuisine. This recipe can be doubled and made a day ahead of serving. It's a crowd pleaser.

Serves 8 to 10

1 c. sautéed mushrooms
5 c. cubed cooked chicken
1/2 c. sliced uncooked scallions
1/4 c. crumbled cooked bacon or 1/2 c. cubed ham
1 t. Mexican oregano
salt and pepper to taste
1 medium onion, chopped
2 jalapeños, seeded and chopped finely
2 cloves garlic, chopped finely
5 T. butter
5 T. flour
3 c. chicken broth

2 c. milk
salt and pepper
pinch of nutmeg
dash of cayenne
8–10 flour tortillas
grated cheddar, Monterey Jack, or a mixture of cheeses

Combine the mushrooms, cooked chicken, scallions, bacon, oregano, salt, and pepper in a bowl.

Make the sauce by sautéing the onions, jalapeños, and garlic in the butter until soft. Add the flour and cook for a few minutes until the sauce is a light golden brown. Add the broth and milk gradually while stirring. Cook and stir over low heat until thickened. Season with salt, pepper, nutmeg, and a dash of cayenne.

To assemble, combine the chicken mixture with enough sauce to bind. Soften the tortillas by grilling on both sides quickly. Dip each tortilla on both sides in sauce, add filling, and roll. Cover the rolled tortillas with the remaining sauce. Sprinkle with cheese and bake for 30 to 35 minutes or until the sauce bubbles.

Groundnut Stew

Long before Julia Child entered our lives via her wonderful books, this was one of our favorite company dishes. It represents a time, the early 1970s, when American cooks were opening up to international influences, partly as a result of the Peace Corps. A friend brought us this recipe from Ghana, where he spent two years as a corps member and, while there, fell in love with African cooking.

Serves 8

2 T. oil
3- to 4–lb. chicken cut into pieces (or 3 lbs. beef stew meat, cut into small chunks)
2 onions, chopped
4–5 medium carrots, thinly sliced
4 cloves garlic, minced

1 T. minced fresh ginger

1 T. chopped fresh jalapeño pepper

1 14-oz. can tomatoes, diced

3 T. tomato paste

5 c. chicken stock or broth

2 t. fresh thyme leaves (or 1 t. dried thyme)

salt and pepper to taste

1 c. smooth natural (unhomogenized) peanut butter

4–6 c. cooked brown or white basmati rice

1/2 c. chopped roasted unsalted peanuts

Heat 2 T. oil in an oven roasting pan. Brown the chicken pieces (or beef cubes) in the oil. Remove the chicken from the pan and set aside. Drain off most of the fat, leaving approximately 2 T. in the pan. Add the onions and sauté for 5 minutes or until soft. Add the carrots, garlic, ginger, and jalapeño. Sauté for 2 minutes longer. Add the tomatoes, tomato paste, 4 c. of the chicken stock, thyme, and salt and pepper.

Bring to a boil, then simmer for 2 to 2 1/2 hours or until chicken or beef is very tender.

In a small saucepan, warm the remaining c. of stock. Add the peanut butter to the stock and stir until well blended. Add the mixture to the stew. Adjust the seasonings, adding Tabasco or another kind of hot chili sauce if you prefer a spicier stew.

While making the stew, cook brown or white basmati rice according to package directions. Serve the stew over the rice and garnish with chopped peanuts.

Cold Roast Chicken with Aioli

Bill and I first tasted aioli, "the butter of Provence," in Carroll Kyser's Carrboro kitchen before we ever set foot in France. To celebrate the arrival of spring, Carroll would prepare a feast of cold chicken, blanched green beans, potatoes, and carrots served with the garlicky mayonnaise. This traditional meal, *le grand aioli* (usually made with salt cod instead of chicken in Provence), is a warm-weather ritual in the mountainous region above Nice, where Carroll spent childhood summers with her family.

Serves 4

2 1/2-lb. chicken
1 stalk celery, broken into 2 or 3 pieces
1 carrot, broken into 2 pieces
3 cloves garlic, peeled
1 lemon, pierced with a fork
fresh thyme and rosemary leaves
olive oil
salt and pepper to taste
aioli (recipe follows)

Salt and pepper the chicken's cavity. Then fill it with the carrot, celery, garlic, lemon, and herbs. Brush the outside of the chicken with olive oil, sprinkle with salt and pepper, and rub additional thyme and rosemary on the skin. Bake at 425° for 10 minutes. The turn the oven to 375° and continue cooking for another hour or more until the juices run clear. Remove the from oven. Discard the vegetables in the cavity.

Let the chicken stand before serving or chill until cold. Serve with aioli and cooked vegetables such as carrots, green beans, and potatoes on the side, all slathered with aioli.

AIOLI

1 head (about 12 cloves) peeled garlic
4 egg yolks
salt to taste
pinch of cumin
1 1/2 c. olive oil

Pound the garlic in a mortar. Add the egg yolks and salt and pound until thick and light yellow. Add a pinch of cumin.

Transfer to a mixing bowl. Gradually whisk in the olive oil in a very thin stream, until thick and very pale. This process can be done in a blender, as you would make mayonnaise, but the texture will not be as authentically unctuous as old-fashioned aioli.

Egg Foo Young

This is one of the very first recipes that Bill and I made together, in the student kitchen of Alspaugh Dormitory at Duke. It was inspired by a meal in our favorite Chinese restaurant in the late 1960s, downtown Durham's The Moon. Infamous back then for its overuse of MSG, The Moon's food often produced a certain throbbing of the heart, not an unpleasant feeling for young lovers.

Egg foo young is currently out of vogue, but recently I noticed it on a Chinese restaurant menu and ordered the dish for purely nostalgic reasons. A little greasy, the restaurant's version didn't make my heart throb, but it stirred up some wonderful memories. Panfried in a little oil, rather than deep-fried, egg foo young is still an appealing omelet and a good way to use leftover meat.

Serves 2

1 c. chopped cooked meat (chicken, pork, or ham)
1/2 c. chopped onion
1 c. bean sprouts, drained
3 T. soy sauce
1 T. salt
3 eggs
peanut oil
foo young sauce (recipe follows)

Mix all of the ingredients except the oil and eggs in a bowl. Add slightly beaten eggs and stir lightly. Panfry in a small amount of oil. Turn over to finish cooking and lift out when brown. Drain on a paper towel.

Right before cooking the omelet, make the sauce. Serve the omelet with the warm sauce poured on top.

FOO YOUNG SAUCE

1 1/2 c. chicken stock
1 t. molasses
1 t. soy sauce
1 T. cornstarch mixed with 2 T. cold water

Mix together all of the ingredients in a small saucepan. Bring to boiling, stirring constantly. Sauce will thicken. Let it simmer 1 minute; then pour it on the omelet.

Lamb Couscous

The first formally trained chef Bill knew personally was Jacques Condoret, who had immigrated to America with his family after training at Château d'Artigny in the Loire valley. By the time we met him, Jacques was executive chef at Hope Valley Country Club in Durham. I applied for a job there and ended up working in "garde manger," which translates rather unglamorously as "the cold kitchen." Fortunately for my artistic inclinations, Jacques encouraged elaborate garniture, and taught me to make "food sculpture" for the club's fancy buffets. At home Bill and I would practice making apple peacocks, melon whales, and tomato roses. Later these decorative techniques would come in handy on our catering jobs.

Bill and I became friends with Jacques and his wife, Nicole, both "pieds noirs," exiled from their beloved Algeria after the civil war in the 1950s. We often visited their home in the country, where we practiced speaking French with Nicole while our toddler Matt played with the Condoret children. We were in awe of Jacques, who made a living doing what we loved to do most, even though he seemed to work eight days a week.

At home it was Nicole who ran the kitchen. She served up a mean couscous, cooked in a simple but exotic contraption called a couscoussier.

A few years later, one of the first pots we bought for our restaurant kitchen was a couscoussier. In it we tried to replicate the traditional Algerian lamb stew with couscous that Nicole had lovingly shared with us along with reminiscences of her childhood in French Algeria.

Serves 8

1/2 c. butter
4 lbs. leg of lamb cut into 1 1/2– to 2-inch cubes
salt and black pepper to taste (at least 1/2 t. each)
1 T. grated fresh ginger
1/4 t. saffron (crushed threads or powder)
1/2 t. turmeric
1 t. or 2 sticks cinnamon
5 whole cloves
1/2 t. freshly grated nutmeg
2 medium onions, halved and cut into inch-thick slices
6–7 c. lamb stock or chicken broth
5 small white turnips, peeled and quartered
4 carrots, peeled and cut into 1-inch slices
1/2 c. raisins
3 medium zucchini, cut into 1/2-inch slices
1 14-oz. can chickpeas, drained
1 lb. couscous
harissa sauce (available in gourmet shops or Middle Eastern groceries)
1/2 c. or more blanched almonds

Melt the butter in a Dutch oven and add the meat, salt, pepper, ginger, saffron, cinnamon, nutmeg, turmeric, and cloves. Over medium heat, turn the meat in the mixture without browning. Add the onions and continue to cook until they are soft but not brown. Add the broth and bring to a simmer. Cover and continue to cook for an hour or until the meat is tender. Add the turnips, carrots, and raisins. Cook 15 minutes longer. Add the zucchini and chickpeas. Cook 5 more minutes or until all vegetables are tender. Adjust seasonings.

Make the couscous according to package directions.

When the couscous is ready, spoon onto each plate individually. Lift the meat and vegetables out of the cooking liquid with a slotted spoon and serve on top of the couscous.

Mix harissa into the broth (taste carefully, a little goes a long way).

At the table, pass the broth separately to spoon over the couscous. Pass the almonds for garnish.

AT HOME

Grits and Grillades

David Perry, coauthor of the *Good Old Grits Cookbook*, gets a look in his eye when speaking about his collaboration with Bill—one corner of his mouth goes up in a half grin that reveals happy memories, but his look betrays a hint of sadness. Clearly he misses his friend and collaborator.

David and his family still cook from *Good Old Grits*. This is the recipe they use most.

Grillade is a Cajun term for a cutlet, a thin boneless slice of pork, veal, or beef.

Serves 4

3 T. bacon fat
3 T. flour
salt and pepper to taste
1 lb. thin pork or veal cutlets, pounded flat
1 c. chopped onions
1/4 c. chopped celery
1/2 c. chopped red or green bell peppers
1 14-oz. can tomatoes, diced, including liquid
pinch of dried red pepper flakes
1 large clove garlic, minced
1/4 c. water
4 servings grits, cooked according to package directions
chopped parsley

Heat the fat in a large skillet over medium-high heat. Mix together the flour, salt, and pepper on a plate. Dip both sides of the cutlets in the mixture. Brown quickly on each side.

Add the onions, celery, and peppers and sauté until tender. Add the tomatoes and their liquid, pepper flakes, garlic, and water. Simmer until the meat is tender, about 20 minutes. Add a little more water if the sauce becomes too thick. Place cooked grits on 4 plates. Top with the grillades and sauce. Garnish with parsley and serve hot.

Grilled Stuffed Quail

Jean Marie Neal told me that her brother's fascination with the entire process of food preparation did not extend to hunting. Though he didn't mind wringing a chicken's neck, shooting game held no appeal for him. In Bill's family, father Frank and brother Tommy did the shooting, but Bill would help clean and dress the birds they brought home for his mother to cook.

This particular quail recipe was inspired by Craig Claiborne's visit to Bill's tiny apartment in 1985. Bill cooked the birds on his flimsy dime-store grill while Mr. Claiborne took notes for his column. Along with muddle (a very thick fish stew) and hoppin' John, the quail dish appeared in "Young Chefs," the *New York Times* article that gave Crook's national exposure and established Bill's reputation as a distinctively Southern chef.

Serves 4

8 cleaned quail, about 1/4 lb. each
1/8 lb. bacon or pork fat cut into small cubes, about 1/2 c.
1 T. finely chopped garlic
3 T. fine dry bread crumbs
3 T. finely diced carrots
3 T. finely diced celery
1 T. finely chopped fresh basil
1 T. finely chopped parsley
1/2 t. finely chopped fresh thyme
salt and black pepper to taste
2 T. vegetable oil

Preheat a charcoal grill until white ashes form on top of the coals.

Split each quail neatly along the backbone. Set aside.

Put the bacon or pork fat and garlic on a flat surface and chop until almost a paste. Put the mixture in a bowl and add the bread crumbs, carrots, celery, herbs, salt, and pepper. Blend thoroughly with the fingers.

Carefully separate by hand a portion of the breast meat from the bone to form a small pocket. Push equal portions of the stuffing into the cavities.

Push any additional stuffing under the skin of the bird without breaking the skin if possible. Brush the birds all over with oil.

Place the quail skin-side down on the grill and cook until nicely browned on one side, 4 to 5 minutes. Carefully turn the halves over and grill 4 to 5 minutes or until done.

Sausage Chez Vous

One of the recipes Bill concocted using his Crook's Corner Cajun Salt, this dish was served for breakfast with "Bible pancakes," so named to persuade neighbors Carroll and Jay to let their children come over to play with Elliott and Madeline on Sunday mornings. They would allow the kids to skip Sunday school only if Bill promised to read the Bible while the kids ate, which he faithfully did.

Makes 8 2-oz. patties

1 lb. fairly lean ground pork
5 t. Crook's Corner Cajun Salt (page 114)
1/4 t. salt

Mix the pork and seasonings well. Shape into patties. Fry over medium-low heat until lightly browned.

DESSERTS AND QUICKBREADS

Biscuits

I can hardly remember a visit to Bill's Carrboro house when biscuits weren't served, morning, noon, and night. (Why wasn't the man fat as a pig?) Ham biscuits were Bill's favorite snack food. He loved to serve them with a barely dry champagne such as White Star—a match made in heaven. No fancy French hors d'oeuvre could have tasted better on a lazy late summer afternoon on his deck.

More than any other dish, biscuits remind the kids of their dad. Served right out of the oven with butter and his homemade strawberry preserves and a glass of cold milk . . . now that's a memory.

If you have trouble with this recipe, I refer you to Bill's *Biscuits, Spoonbread, and Sweet Potato Pie*. He devotes two pages to the basics of biscuit making and extols the virtues of "soft Southern (low-gluten) flour," which is, according to Bill, the secret of good biscuits. He even offers the address of White Lily Kitchens, from which you can order "the absolutely best flour for biscuits."

Makes about 24 small biscuits

2 c. low-gluten flour, such as White Lily or Martha White
heaping 1/2 t. salt
3 1/4 t. baking powder
1/2 t. baking soda (only if using buttermilk)
5 T. chilled shortening, lard, or butter, or a combination
7/8 c. whole milk (or buttermilk)

Preheat oven to 500°.

Sift the dry ingredients together into a large bowl. Add the cold shortening and work all through the flour using the fingertips. Every bit of flour should be combined with a bit of fat. Add the milk, or buttermilk, and stir just until dry ingredients are incorporated and the dough forms a ball, being careful not to overwork it.

Turn the dough out onto a lightly floured surface. Knead lightly for about 10 strokes or until the dough begins to look smooth.

Pat or roll the dough out into a rectangle, about 3/4 inch high. Cut into 2-inch rounds. Place on an ungreased cookie sheet and bake in the preheated oven for 8 minutes, or until lightly browned.

For cheese biscuits, add 1 1/2 c. cheddar cheese to the dough after the milk.

Serve hot with butter.

Bill with his family in Grover, North Carolina, 1985.

Bill at home in Carrboro, 1988.

Fried Pies

After siblings Jean Marie, Bill, and Tommy spent the day helping Daddy Neal tend the crops, Mama Neal rewarded them with fried pies. Jean Marie recalls seeing Bill standing on the porch, eye-level with the table where the pies were placed to cool, impatient for his grandmother's permission to dig in.

Makes about 12 pies

1 recipe biscuit dough (page 197)
jam or preserves (preferably homemade)
fat for frying (oil, shortening, or lard, or a combination)
powdered sugar

Roll out the biscuit dough to a thickness of 3/4 inch. Cut into 2-inch rounds. Roll each round into a circle, about 5 inches in diameter. In the center, put a T. of jam. Moisten the edges with a little water. Fold over the dough to form a half circle. Press together the edges with a fork.

Add enough fat in a heavy skillet to reach a depth of 1/4 to 1/2 inch. Fry the pies over medium heat until light brown. Turn to fry the other side.

Drain the pies on paper towels. Sprinkle with powdered sugar and serve immediately.

Piecrust

Bill's sister Jean Marie remembered his instructions to use three kinds of fat in piecrust: butter for flavor, shortening for tenderness, lard for flakiness. If you can't find lard—and it's scarce nowadays even in the Deep South—use equal parts butter and vegetable shortening, but you'll miss the divine flakiness that good old pig fat imbues.

Food processors didn't exist, of course, when Mama Neal made piecrust. But at home Bill was a food processor enthusiast.

Makes 2 bottom crusts or 1 double crust

2 c. White Lily or all-purpose flour
1 t. salt
2/3 c. cold lard or shortening or a mixture of lard, shortening, and butter
1/3 c. cold water

Hand method: Sift together the flour and salt into a mixing bowl. Divide the fat into several chunks. Using two knives, a pastry blender, or your finger tips, cut in the fat one chunk at a time until the dough resembles coarse cornmeal. Do not overwork the dough. Sprinkle in the water and work it into the dough with a fork, just enough to bind.

Processor method: Blend salt and flour in a food processor bowl. Add the fat in large chunks, pulsing for a few seconds after each has been put in. Process until the mixture resembles course meal. Add water. Pulse just 1 to 2 seconds more until the dough sticks together.

On a smooth, floured surface, form the dough into a ball. Mash with the heel of your hand and knead 4 or 5 times. Divide into 2 balls, wrap in plastic, and chill for at least 1/2 hour.

Roll out on a floured surface to a thickness of about 1/8 inch. Turn an ungreased pie dish upside down and place in the middle of the rolled dough. Cut the dough into a circle 2 1/2 inches wider than the outer rim of the pie plate. Holding the dough circle inside the pie dish with one hand, carefully flip the pie plate and dough right-side up.

For a single-crust pie, fold the outside of the circle over to create a rim on the outer surface of the pie plate. With a fork or with a thumb and two fingers, crimp the rim.

To bake a crust to be filled later, cover the pie shell with aluminum foil. Add a pound of rice or dry beans to weigh down the crust. Bake at 375° for 10 minutes. Remove the foil and bake 5 minutes more or until the crust is golden brown.

For a double-crust pie, fill the bottom crust. Lay the second circle on top of the filling and cut to fit. Crimp together the bottom and top crusts. Make several slashes in the top crust for steam to escape or cut a decorative design in it. Bake according to the pie recipe instructions.

Chocolate Chess Pie

On summer Saturdays Bill entertained the children and their friends Amanda and Taylor by setting up a bake-sale stand on his corner of old Carrboro. This little ritual was eagerly anticipated by the neighbors, who began to depend on this service for their weekend dinner parties.

The kids helped put together lemon and chocolate chess pies the night before, and then manned the "store." As soon as the last pie was sold, they hightailed it down to nearby Nice Price Books, where they inevitably spent all the profits on recycled comic books.

This pie, which appeared regularly on the dinner tables of many Carrboro mill-town families, appeared in *Biscuits, Spoonbread, and Sweet Potato Pie*, but it is so delicious that the recipe bears repeating. It's irresistible served warm with whipped cream.

Serves 8

2 oz. unsweetened chocolate
1/2 c. butter
4 eggs
1 1/4 c. sugar
1/4 t. salt
2 T. all-purpose flour
2 T. heavy cream
1 1/2 t. vanilla
1 T. bourbon or rum
1 partially baked 9-inch pie shell

Melt the butter and chocolate together over very low heat or in a microwave. Let cool to room temperature. Beat the eggs lightly. Toss the sugar, salt, and flour together and stir into the eggs. Add the cream, melted chocolate and butter, vanilla, and whiskey. Mix well.

Pour into the partially baked pie shell. Bake at 325° for about 35 minutes or until the custard is set in the middle and has a slightly crusty top without excess puffing.

French Silk Pie

This is Bill's adaptation of a sinfully rich recipe found all over the South in small-town cookbooks from the 1950s. This may fall in the category of beef Stroganoff, neither French nor particularly Southern, but it was a common dessert of our childhoods. To make that version, prebake a piecrust (page 201). When cool, spoon in the filling, and chill. Serve topped with whipped cream.

At the Chapel Hill Country Club, Bill gussied it up by serving it in individual meringue shells, an adaptation of *dacquoise au chocolat*.

Serves 8

MERINGUE SHELLS

1/2 c. finely chopped pecans
2/3 c. egg whites, room temperature
1/4 t. salt
dash of cream of tartar
1 c. sugar
1 t. vanilla

Toast the pecans.

Butter and flour a cookie sheet.

With an electric mixer, whip the egg whites, salt, and cream of tartar together until foamy. Very gradually add the sugar, beating constantly. When the meringue is firm and not grainy, add the vanilla. Fold in the nuts.

Spoon the meringue mixture into round shapes, about 3 inches in diameter, using the back of the spoon to create an indentation in the middle of each.

Bake at 225° for about 1 hour, checking often. The meringue should remain light colored. If it begins to turn golden, lower the oven temperature and continue to cook until the meringue is crisp and dry.

1 square unsweetened baking chocolate
1 stick (1/2 c.) butter
3/4 c. sugar
1/2 t. vanilla
pinch of salt
2 eggs, unbeaten
sweetened whipped cream
chocolate shavings

Melt the chocolate in a double boiler and allow it to cool to room temperature. Cream the butter, gradually adding the sugar and beating well until quite fluffy. Stir in the melted chocolate, vanilla, and salt. Add the eggs, one at a time, beating at low speed for 5 minutes after each addition. Pour the filling into the cooled meringue shell. Chill. Decorate with sweetened whipped cream and chocolate shavings before serving.

Villa Teo Pecan Pie

This pie was one of the most popular deserts served at the Villa Teo in the early 1970s, and the only recipe I still have from that era. I retrieved it from the personal cookbook I compiled in high school. Most likely, its provenance is a 1960s-era women's magazine—the winner of a Philadelphia Cream Cheese recipe contest or something of that sort.

This mongrel dessert, half pecan pie–half cheesecake, was fairly typical of American cooking of that time. It was not at all representative of Bill's later cooking style, as he evolved into something of a purist, but he absolutely adored this dessert and enjoyed it at home throughout his life.

I think it's best served warm topped with whipped cream.

Serves 8

8 oz. cream cheese
1/3 c. sugar
1 egg

3 more eggs
1/4 c. sugar
1/2 t. salt
1 t. vanilla
1 c. dark Karo Syrup
1 uncooked pie shell
1 1/4 c. coarsely chopped pecans

Preheat oven to 375°.

Cream together the cream cheese and 1/3 c. sugar. Add 1 egg and beat until well mixed.

In another small bowl, beat the next 5 ingredients (3 eggs, 1/4 c. sugar, salt, vanilla, and Karo syrup) until well blended.

Spread the cream cheese mixture evenly on the bottom of the uncooked pie shell. Top with the pecans. Pour the syrup mixture over the pecans. Bake for 35 to 40 minutes or until the middle of the pie is puffy and no longer jiggles.

Aunt Lily's Coffee Cake

As far as I know, Bill had no relative named Lily. My theory is that he named this recipe for White Lily, the brand of low-gluten "soft" flour both his grandmothers used to make the flakiest piecrusts and fluffiest biscuits, as well as delicately crumbed cakes like this one.

Serves 8 to 12

TOPPING

1/3 c. firmly packed brown sugar
2 T. sugar
1 c. walnuts or pecans
1 1/2 t. cinnamon
1/2 c. cake flour
4 T. butter
1/2 t. vanilla

Coarsely chop the nuts and toss with the sugars and cinnamon in a small mixing bowl. Set aside about 3/4 c. of the mixture to use as a filling. In the remainder, rapidly cut in flour, butter, and vanilla. Do not overblend. The mixture should have a rough, crumbly texture.

CAKE

4 egg yolks
2/3 c. sour cream
1 1/2 t. vanilla
2 c. sifted White Lily flour (substitute cake flour if you must)
1 c. sugar
1/2 t. baking powder
1/2 t. baking soda
1/2 t. salt
6 T. (3 oz.) butter, softened
2 c. blueberries, blackberries, or coarsely chopped peaches

Preheat oven to 350°. Butter well a 9 1/2-inch springform pan.

Put the yolks, 1/4 of the sour cream, and vanilla in a medium-sized mixing bowl. Whisk until smooth.

Sift the flour, sugar, baking powder, baking soda, and salt into a large mixing bowl. Stir in the butter and the rest of the sour cream until the mixture is moist. Beat for 1 1/2 minutes in an electric mixer. Gradually add the egg mixture in 3 batches, beating for 20 seconds after each addition.

Scoop 2/3 of the batter into the greased springform pan. Smooth the surface. Sprinkle with the reserved filling of nuts, sugars, and cinnamon and the fruit of your choice. Pour the rest of the batter on top and smooth over. Add the crumb topping.

Bake at 350° for about 55 to 65 minutes. If the top gets too brown, loosely cover with aluminum foil. Use a clean straw to test for doneness. Any fruit drawn out may be wet, but the crumb topping should be firm and set. Serve warm.

Date Nut Cake

Bill first tasted this old-fashioned cake at my grandmother Hobbs's house in Mississippi; it was a recipe from her childhood. We made it in my dormitory kitchen using the recipe from *Cooks from Ole Brook*, my hometown ladies' club cookbook. Once we had a kitchen of our own, we baked it often, but after opening La Résidence we abandoned it for fancier gâteaux.

For years I forgot about this cake, and recipes using dates seem to have gone out of vogue; but recently I bumped into the same family recipe in *Southern Living*. It won first prize in the magazine's holiday cook-off! I was delighted to see that this old relic is undergoing a revival.

Serves 12 or more

1 c. salted butter, room temperature
2 c. sugar
4 egg yolks, room temperature
3 c. flour
1 t. baking soda
1 1/3 c. buttermilk
1 c. chopped pecans
1 package dates, chopped
4 egg whites
orange glaze (recipe follows)

Grease and flour an 8- to 9-inch tube or Bundt pan.

Prepare the orange glaze and set aside while you make the cake batter.

For the cake, beat the butter and add sugar gradually until fluffy. Add the egg yolks, one at a time, beating well between additions.

Sift the flour and baking soda. Mix into the butter mixture in thirds alternately with the buttermilk. Stir in the pecans and dates.

Beat the egg whites until stiff peaks form. Fold the whites carefully into the cake batter and pour into the pan.

Bake at 325° for 1 1/2 hours. Let the cake sit for at least 5 minutes before carefully unmolding onto a plate. While still warm, punch several holes into the top of the cake with a skewer. Slowly pour the orange glaze onto the cake, allowing it to seep into the holes. Let the cake rest and absorb the glaze for at least 1/2 hour before serving.

ORANGE GLAZE

1 c. orange juice
2 c. granulated sugar
2 T. grated orange rind

Mix all of the ingredients. Allow to rest for at least an hour before pouring onto the cake, stirring a few times to dissolve the sugar. The mixture should be a little grainy, so don't worry if the sugar doesn't completely dissolve.

Pineapple Upside-Down Cake

Minus the bourbon, this is the same upside-down cake most baby boomers grew up eating. The children loved it as much as Bill and I did. Bill made this at home and also served it at Crook's, using the Dole Pineapple Company's original recipe popularized in the 1950s. He added the hooch, a nice grown-up touch.

Serves 8

1 stick (1/2 c.) salted butter
1 c. sugar
2 eggs
1 t. vanilla extract
1 1/2 c. all-purpose flour
1/4 t. salt
3/4 t. baking powder
1/4 t. baking soda
1/2 c. buttermilk or yogurt
6 T. salted butter
3/4 c. light brown sugar
2 T. bourbon
1 14-oz. can sliced pineapple rings

In a medium-sized mixing bowl, cream the butter until fluffy. Gradually add the sugar, beating all the while. Add the eggs, one at a time, beating after each addition just enough to blend thoroughly. Add the vanilla. Sift together the flour, salt, baking powder, and baking soda. Add the flour in thirds to the creamed mixture, alternating with buttermilk. Blend well after each addition, careful not to overbeat, as this will toughen the cake.

For the topping, place the butter in a 9 x 2-inch round pan on top of a stove burner set on low. When the butter is melted, stir in the brown sugar and bourbon, mixing evenly. The sugar-butter mixture should cover the bottom of the pan.

Drain the canned pineapple. Chop two of the slices coarsely. Slice the remaining rings in two. Arrange the pineapple slices in a circle covering the bottom of the pan and sprinkle with the chopped pineapple.

Bake at 350° for 45 to 50 minutes or until the cake pulls away from the side of the pan. Immediately place a cake plate on top of the cake pan and invert the pan. Leave the pan inverted on the plate for about 5 minutes before carefully removing it. Serve warm or room temperature with whipped cream.

Vanity Cake

Although this recipe appears in *Biscuits, Spoonbread, and Sweet Potato Pie*, it bears repeating. My grandmother served vanity cake to Bill on his first visit to Mississippi, and he fell in love with it. Bill made it repeatedly for the Chapel Hill Country Club, and later it became a regular dessert for many years at both La Résidence and Crook's.

Experienced bakers will recognize the familiar 1-2-3-4 cake recipe, surely the most popular yellow cake of the twentieth century.

Serves 12 to 15

3 c. cake flour, sifted
4 t. baking powder
1/2 t. salt
2 sticks (1 c.) butter at room temperature

2 c. sugar
4 eggs at room temperature
1 t. vanilla extract
1 c. milk at room temperature
vanity cake filling (recipe follows)
sifted powdered sugar or sweetened whipped cream

Preheat oven to 350°. Butter and flour 3 9-inch cake pans. Sift together the flour, baking powder, and salt.

With an electric mixer, cream the butter and sugar until the mixture is light yellow and fluffy.

Add the eggs, one at a time, beating thoroughly after each goes into the mixture. Add the vanilla extract.

Beat in the flour alternately with the milk, beginning and ending with the flour until well mixed, being careful not to overbeat.

Pour the batter into the prepared cake pans and bake for 30 minutes or until the sides of the cake draw away from the pans and a straw stuck into the center of the cake comes out clean.

Cool for 5 minutes before inverting the layers on a cake rack. Allow to cool to room temperature before filling.

VANITY CAKE FILLING

2 eggs
1 c. sugar
2 1/4 c. grated apples (about 2 large)
juice and grated zest of 1 lemon
2 T. butter
pinch of salt

In a heavy nonaluminum saucepan, whisk the eggs and sugar until they are well mixed. Add the remaining ingredients. Cook on very low heat, stirring constantly. The filling will begin to steam before the mixture thickens and coats a spoon. Immediately remove from heat and transfer to a bowl. Cool.

To compose the cake, spread the filling on top of the bottom and middle layers. On the top layer, sprinkle sifted confectioners' sugar, or spread with whipped cream. If using whipped cream, you will need to refrigerate the cake immediately.

Lemon Cake Pudding

During the hiatus between our leaving Fearrington and opening the new space in Chapel Hill, Georgia Kyser—truly our fairy godmother—invited all four of us (including brand-new baby Elliott) to stay at her Franklin Street home. Days were spent decorating the new place with Georgia's invaluable help; evenings we all cooked dinner together.

Here is Georgia's recipe for a quick dessert she would make at the spur of the moment, and we never tired of eating it.

Serves 6

1 c. sugar
1/4 c. flour
1/4 t. salt
3 eggs, separated
1 1/2 c. milk, scalded
5 T. lemon juice
1 T. grated lemon zest
2 T. melted butter
1/2 c. toasted slivered almonds (optional)
hot water

For this dish you will need a baking pan big enough to hold a 1 1/2-qt. shallow casserole or gratin dish. Grease the casserole. Preheat oven to 350°.

Mix together the sugar, flour, and salt.

Beat the egg yolks until thick. Add the milk, lemon juice and zest, and melted butter. Lightly whisk together the dry ingredients and the egg yolk mixture, just until well mixed.

Beat the egg whites until stiff peaks form. Fold the egg whites carefully into the batter.

Pour the batter into the greased casserole dish. Place the casserole in the larger pan. Gently pour hot water into the pan halfway up the side of the casserole; place in the oven. Sprinkle the pudding with almonds if you like.

Bake for 45 to 50 minutes until puffed and golden. Serve warm or at room temperature.

Peaches, Berries, and Dumplings

In an unpublished manuscript, Bill wrote, "The peach I remember from my childhood for pies and cobblers and any sort of baking was the white-fleshed and ruby-hearted Belle of Georgia. You can use whatever peach is sweet and fresh at your market. Though it pains me to say it, frozen sliced peaches are quite often better than what you'll find on the green grocer's shelf."

Serves 6

4 c. peeled, sliced peaches
1 c. fresh blackberries or blueberries
2 1/2 c. water
1–1 1/2 c. sugar
small pinch of cinnamon
drop dumplings (recipe follows)
whipped cream

Combine the fruits, water, sugar to taste (tart blackberries require more sweetener than blueberries), and cinnamon in a heavy-bottomed saucepan. Bring to a rapid boil, reduce heat, and simmer until just tender. Do not over-cook.

Drop the dumpling batter by the spoonful into the simmering fruit. Cover and cook about 6 to 8 minutes, or until the dumplings are light and done through. Serve the dish warm or at room temperature, with a small dollop of whipped cream if desired.

DROP DUMPLINGS

1 c. all-purpose flour
1 1/2 t. baking powder

1/2 t. baking soda
1/4 t. salt
1 1/2 t. sugar
1 egg separated
1/2 c. plus 2 T. nonfat buttermilk
1 T. melted butter

Sift the dry ingredients together into a mixing bowl.

Beat the egg yolk with the buttermilk and the melted butter. Stir gently into the flour.

Beat the egg white until soft peaks form. Fold into the batter. Use immediately.

Blueberry Banana Muffins

In blueberry season, Bill liked to make these muffins and freeze them. On mornings when neighbors popped over for a garden stroll and coffee on the deck, he would heat them for a few minutes and serve. This recipe will make 12 regular-sized muffins, though he preferred to use miniature muffin tins for fast thawing.

Makes 12 large or 24 miniature muffins

1 1/2 c. all-purpose flour
2 1/4 t. baking powder
1/2 t. baking soda
1/3 c. sugar
1 egg
3/4 c. buttermilk
1/3 c. mashed ripe banana
1/4 c. melted butter
1/2 c. chopped pecans
1/2 c. blueberries

Preheat oven to 400°. Sift the flour, baking powder, baking soda, and sugar into a large bowl.

Beat the egg with the buttermilk and mashed banana. Stir into the dry ingredients along with the melted butter. Fold in the pecans and the blueberries.

Spoon the mixture into 24 well-buttered miniature muffin tins. Bake for about 15 to 18 minutes or until the tops are golden (several minutes longer for large muffins). Let cool a few minutes; then turn out. Serve warm.

Georgia's Gingerbread

Here's another old-fashioned recipe, a classic that bears reviving.

Serves 9 to 12

1/4 lb. butter
1 c. sugar
2 eggs
3/4 c. boiling water
3/4 c. molasses
2 1/2 c. flour
2 t. baking soda
1 1/2 t. salt
lemon sauce (recipe follows) or sweetened whipped cream

Grease and flour a 9 x 9-inch square pan. Cream the butter, add the sugar, and beat until light and fluffy. Add the eggs and beat well. Add the boiling water and molasses and blend. Sift together the dry ingredients and add to the batter.

Bake at 350° for 35 to 45 minutes. Serve warm, cut into squares, topped with lemon sauce or whipped cream.

LEMON SAUCE

3/4 c. sugar
pinch of salt
2 T. cornstarch
1 1/2 c. boiling water

3 T. butter
2 t. lemon rind
4 T. lemon juice

In a heavy-bottomed saucepan, combine the sugar, salt, and cornstarch. Stir in the boiling water gradually. Cook, stirring constantly, until thick. Lightly beat the egg yolks together. Gradually stir the sugar mixture into the beaten egg yolks. Pour back into the saucepan and cook just a minute or two until the sauce thickens a bit more. Remove from heat and immediately add the butter, lemon juice, and rind. As the butter melts, stir in thoroughly to incorporate. Cool to room temperature before serving.

Nut Shortbread

Bill's first trip to Mississippi was during the Christmas holidays of 1970. As he had done every year since I was seven or so, my father, Henry Hobbs, took a group of my siblings and cousins caroling around the neighborhood. Bill happily joined the fun—and replaced my father as accompanist when we returned for the final concert at my grandmother's house.

One of our stops was a family friend named Mrs. Vernon. Bill was fascinated by the grand piano that dominated her living room. On top of this piano was a silver urn full of white peacock feathers. Mrs. Vernon raised peacocks, including the rare white ones, and was rumored to spoil her pets by feeding them homemade shortbread every day. After our concert Mrs. Vernon gave us a tin full of these cookies, all shaped by the same scalloped-edged cookie cutter. In comparison with other holiday sweets, decorated with green and red icing and sugar sprinkles, these cookies seemed to us the height of elegance and simplicity.

After we married, making shortbread became one of our Christmas rituals. This is not exactly Mrs. Vernon's recipe—the nuts would probably have given the peacocks indigestion—but one Bill developed later and served at Crook's.

2 c. flour
1/4 c. cornstarch
1/2 c. sugar
1/2 t. salt
1/2 lb. butter
2 egg yolks
1/2 t. vanilla extract
2 t. water
1 c. finely chopped walnuts, pecans, or almonds

Stir together the dry ingredients. With a pastry cutter or two knives, cut in the butter until the mixture is crumbly. Quickly stir in the egg yolks, lightly beaten with the vanilla and 2 t. water. Stir in the nuts. Knead the dough lightly and rapidly. If it seems too soft to roll, add a little flour. Chill the dough.

Roll the dough out on a lightly floured surface to a thickness of about 1/3 inch. Cut with cookie cutters in desired shapes—preferably scalloped-edged rounds! Bake on an ungreased sheet for 20 minutes at 375°. Cool on a rack.

Jelly Tarts

Years before La Résidence was even a gleam in our eyes, each Christmas Bill and I made an assortment of cookies to give friends. Staples were seafoam (a version of divinity candy made with brown sugar), chocolate bourbon balls aged at least a week for proper mellowing, and jelly tarts, also known as thumbprint cookies. These treats offered the full spectrum of our favorite holiday ingredients: pecans, caramel, chocolate, colorful fruit, booze, and lots of butter.

The cookies melt in your mouth. They look like colorful little jewels, and taste even better than they look.

Makes at least 4 dozen cookies

1 c. salted butter
1/4 c. sugar
pinch of salt
3 c. flour
assorted flavors of jelly, not jam or preserves

Cream the butter with the sugar until fluffy. Add salt. Gradually blend in the flour, until a fairly stiff dough is formed. For each tart, pinch off a piece of dough, enough to form a ball about 1 inch in diameter. With your thumb, make an indentation in each cookie. Place on an ungreased cookie sheet and fill the indentation with jelly. Bake at 325° for 20 minutes or until the cookies barely begin to color.

Toffee Bars

Everybody loved these cookies. Until we opened our own restaurant, we must have made them once a week.

Makes 4 dozen cookies

1 c. salted butter
1 c. brown sugar
2 c. flour
1/2 t. salt
1 t. vanilla extract
1 c. chocolate chips or chunks
1 c. chopped pecans

Cream together the butter and sugar until fluffy. Add the vanilla. Add the flour and salt, mixing well, but do not overbeat. Stir in the chocolate and pecans. Mash the dough onto an ungreased jelly roll pan or cookie sheet to a thickness of 1/4 to 1/2 inch. Bake at 350° for about 20 minutes or until golden brown.

Place the pan on a rack for a minute or two before slicing the bars into rectangles. Carefully transfer the bars to paper towels spread out on the counter to cool completely. Do not allow the cookies to remain in the pan too long before cutting or the cookies will crumble.

Bananas Foster

Named for a banana-loving patron of Brennan's Restaurant in New Orleans, bananas Foster, along with its flaming cousin crêpes suzette, was a show-off dessert in the 1960s and '70s, appearing on Continental-style restaurant menus throughout the country. When you ordered bananas Foster, you got not only a delicious dessert but also an impressive floor show.

Steve Levitas, now a Raleigh attorney, was a line cook at the original La Résidence at Fearrington during the two years we lived above the restaurant. He recalled planning a birthday dinner for me, intending to show off his skills by serving bananas Foster as the grand finale. The trick is, of course, to keep the dish aflame until your audience is appropriately impressed. Steve got that part right, but in his moment of triumph the pan began to rotate on its handle, splashing its burning contents all over himself and the floor. He succeeded in making quite an impression on everyone at the table.

When you make this, don't forget to check your sauté pan's handle and keep a fire extinguisher nearby.

For 1 serving

1 ripe banana
2 T. brown sugar
1 T. butter
dash of cinnamon
1 T. banana liqueur
2 T. white rum
1 scoop vanilla ice cream

Cut the banana in half lengthwise, then again crosswise to make 4 pieces.

Melt the butter with the brown sugar and cinnamon in a flat pan or a chafing dish over the stove. Add the banana pieces and sauté for a few minutes until the banana is thoroughly heated. Pour in the liqueur and rum and light with a match. Baste the banana with the flaming liquid until it burns out. To serve, spoon the banana pieces over the ice cream and pour the sauce on top.

Peanut Brittle

Bill and Jean Marie's favorite chore on Daddy and Mama Neal's farm was harvesting peanuts, The kids gobbled up raw almost as many peanuts as they dug up, but there were plenty left for roasted peanuts and peanut brittle, a fall tradition. The siblings loved making the candy, not so much for the taste but for the thrill of seeing the peanuts pop as the candy finished cooking.

Take care while making this candy to avoid being spattered with hot liquid, the element of danger that made this project such fun for the Neal children.

Makes about 1 1/2 lbs.

1 1/4 c. sugar
3/4 c. light corn syrup
4 T. water
1/2 t. salt
2 1/2 c. raw peanuts, skins on
4 T. butter
3/4 t. baking soda

In a large, heavy saucepan, combine the sugar, syrup, water, and salt. Stir occasionally until the mixture boils. Add the peanuts. Boil and stir until the mixture reaches the hard-crack stage, or 295° on a candy thermometer. Remove from heat. Immediately add the baking soda and butter, which will make the candy foam up, then settle down. Pour the mixture onto a greased baking sheet, spread it out, and let cool before breaking into pieces.

Ambrosia

This is a whole different animal than the fruit-and-coconut mixture served all over the South for dessert after a rich Christmas dinner. This version of ambrosia is a champagne cocktail that has been served at Antoine's in New Orleans for at least a century. It tasted just as good at our Carrboro apartment.

For 1 drink

3/4 oz. brandy, chilled
3/4 oz. Cointreau or Grand Marnier, chilled
champagne or other dry sparkling wine

Pour the chilled brandy and Cointreau into a champagne glass and fill with champagne.

Christian Science Punch

When we catered for Bill's graduate school professors and their wives, this punch was popular at ladies' teas, weddings, and dessert parties. Called "Almond Punch" in the old *Chapel Hill Cookbook*, its nickname came from Kay Kyser's family (Kay had left show business to become a Christian Science practitioner in Chapel Hill) to indicate the drink's appropriateness for teetotalers, or maybe to warn those looking for a stronger libation away from it.

Serves 20 to 24

2 c. sugar
1 qt. water
3 lemons
2 c. strong tea
1 t. vanilla
1 t. almond flavoring

1 48-oz. can pineapple juice
1 qt. ginger ale

Squeeze the juice from the lemons. Boil together the sugar, water, and the entire lemon rinds. Add the tea, pineapple juice, lemon juice, and flavorings. Strain. Chill. When ready to serve, pour in the ginger ale.

Christmas Parade Hot Chocolate

Like most Southern towns, Chapel Hill–Carrboro holds a Christmas parade as soon as the town decorations are up. Back when our kids were small, "winter holidays" were still referred to as "the Christmas season," and town decorations were lighted wreaths and bells instead of the politically correct snowflakes that flank Franklin Street now.

Each year on the Saturday morning of the parade, Bill took our three and their best buddies to watch the parade at Crook's. They climbed up on the roof and perched alongside folk artist Clyde Jones's painted animals, the perfect place to take in the festivities below. Bill kept the children warmed up from the inside with this cocoa, or as Madeline remembers it, "the best hot chocolate in the world."

Serves 10 to 12

10 oz. unsweetened chocolate
2 c. hot water
2 qts. half-and-half
2 qts. milk
1 1/2 c. sugar
1/2 t. salt
3 t. vanilla
whipped cream
semisweet chocolate shavings

In the top of a double boiler melt the chocolate in the water, stirring frequently.

Over low heat, scald the cream and milk in a large pot. Stir the sugar and salt into the milk. Then stir the hot milk mixture into the melted chocolate, beating constantly.

Add the vanilla.

Top with whipped cream and chocolate shavings.

Sazerac

The Sazerac is another drink you don't bump into much outside New Orleans. Bill ordered it every time we visited Brennan's in the French Quarter or Commander's Palace when it was a quiet Garden District neighborhood restaurant—before Emeril Lagasse put it on the map.

For 1 drink

1 1/2 oz. rye or bourbon
1 1/2 t. sugar
3 dashes of Peychaud's Bitters (substitute Angostura bitters)
1 T. Herbsaint (substitute Pernod or other anise-flavored liqueur)
one lemon twist

Pour all of the ingredients except the lemon twist in a cocktail shaker filled with crushed ice. Strain into a chilled cocktail glass, add the twist, and serve.

Shirley Temple

Before the current era of political correctness, a Shirley Temple was a sort of training cocktail for kids. When the extended family gathered after church or in the evenings, Shirley Temples were served next to the grown-ups' drinks, usually old-fashioneds, manhattans, or sidecars. The idea was to mirror the adult drink so that the kids wouldn't feel cheated. If the adults were having sherry, a small stemmed glass was used, if a highball, a tall glass with "rocks."

Bill grew up in a dry household, but he made up for lost time as an adult.

When he served cocktails or champagne (his cocktail of choice), the children were offered Shirley Temples in the appropriate glasses.

I'm not sure kids know who Shirley Temple is anymore. Nowadays, I guess this would be called a Barney or a Big Bird.

For 1 drink

ginger ale to fill the glass
dash of grenadine
1 maraschino cherry
1 slice of orange for garnish

Pour chilled ginger ale into the appropriate glass—the prettier the glass, the more elegant the cocktail. Use ice if mimicking a "highball." Add a dash or two of grenadine and the cherry. Slit the orange slice to the middle, and perch it on the rim of the glass to serve.

Sidecar

Bill enjoyed the Sunday dinner ritual at my grandmother Moreton's Mississippi home. As soon as the adults arrived from the church service, sherry or cocktails would be passed on silver trays. Sidecars were a special thrill because of the sugary rim. Bill loved this festive drink and would be delighted that the sidecar has seen a bit of a revival in recent times.

For 1 drink

1 oz. Cointreau
1 oz. lemon juice
1 oz. brandy
lemon juice
sugar

Pour the first 3 ingredients into a cocktail shaker filled with crushed ice. Shake and strain into a stemmed glass prepared by dipping the rim in lemon juice and then in sugar, or simply pour the ingredients into a lowball glass with ice and stir.

Index

Aioli, 191–92
Ambrosia, 220
Appetizers
  artichokes Basquaise, 11–12
  artichokes with goat cheese and
    mustard vinaigrette, 106–7
  artichokes with tomato fennel sauce, 13
  asparagus and shrimp Dijonnaise,
    15–16
  asparagus with rosemary mayonnaise,
    13–14
  beet and endive salad, 16–17
  celeriac rémoulade, 17–18
  chicken liver mousse, 21–22
  corn chips with guacamole and salsa
    cruda, 160–61
  country pâté, 22–25
  deviled eggs, 161–62
  gnocchi verdi with 2 sauces, 18–20
  hors d'oeuvres variés platter, 10–11
  leek gratin, 20–21
  oysters Rockefeller, 163–64
  pimento cheese and crackers, 105
  pissaladière, 25–26
  wild mushroom sauté, 162–63
Apples
  apple celeriac soup, 27
  tarte tatin, 76–77
Artichokes
  artichokes basquaise, 11–12
  artichokes with goat cheese and
    mustard vinaigrette, 106–7

artichokes with tomato fennel sauce,
  13
Asparagus
  asparagus and shrimp Dijonnaise,
    15–16
  asparagus with brown butter and
    capers, 37–38
  asparagus with rosemary mayonnaise,
    13–14
Aunt Lily's coffee cake, 205–6

Backyard spinach pie, 175–76
Bananas
  bananas Foster, 218–19
  blueberry banana muffins, 213–14
Béchamel sauce, 20
Beef
  beef carbonade, 184–85
  boeuf en daube Provençale, 55–56
  Cajun steak, 138
  filet mignon with composed butter,
    53–55
  mustard lover's steak, 139
  vegetable beef soup, 170–71
Beets
  beet and cucumber soup, 166–67
  beet and endive salad, 16–17
Beverages
  ambrosia, 220
  Christian Science punch, 220–21
  Christmas parade hot chocolate,
    221–22

peaches, berries, and dumplings,
212–13
Peanuts
  peanut brittle, 219
  peanut carrot soup, 168–69
Pear cranberry pie, 144
Pebbly mustard sauce, 129
Pecan pie
  Bourbon pecan pie, 145
  Villa Teo pecan pie, 204–5
Persimmon pudding, 149–50
Piecrust, 200–201
Pies
  backyard spinach pie, 175–76
  bourbon pecan pie, 145
  chocolate chess pie, 202
  crab pie, 177–78
  French silk pie, 203–4
  fried pies, 200
  pear cranberry pie, 144
  Princess Pamela's buttermilk pie,
    145–46
  sweet potato pie, 146–47
  Vidalia onion pie, 176–77
  Villa Teo pecan pie, 204–5
Pimento cheese and crackers, 105
Pineapple upside-down cake, 208–9
Pissaladière, 25–26
Polenta, 137
Pompano Pontchartrain, 181
Pork
  braised pork chops with baby limas
    and whole garlic, 136–37
  braised pork with bourbon and prunes,
    67–68
  country-style roast ribs, 137–38
  sausage chez vous, 197
Potatoes
  Edwina's potato salad, 174–75
  La Res potatoes, 39–40

turned potatoes, 40
whipped potatoes, 125
See also Sweet potatoes
Princess Pamela's buttermilk pie, 145–46
Puddings
  bread pudding, 147–49
  cabbage pudding, 171–73
  lemon cake pudding, 211–12
  persimmon pudding, 149–50
Pumpkin soup, 169–70
Punch, Christian Science, 220–21

Quail, grilled stuffed, 195–96
Queen of Sheba cake, 74–76
Quick black bean soup, 167–68

Ratatouille, 41–42
Ravigote sauce, 34–35
Red slaw, 125
Ribs, country-style roast, 137–38
Rice, dirty, 122
Roquefort walnut butter, 55
Rosemary mayonnaise, 13–14
Rouille, 35–36
Roulades
  chocolate roulade, 79–80
  walnut roulade, 80–82

Sabayon, Grand Marnier, 91
Salade Niçoise, 183–84
Salads
  beet and endive salad, 16–17
  East Carolina coleslaw, 173–74
  Edwina's potato salad, 174–75
  grated carrot salad, 39
  red slaw, 125
  salade Niçoise, 183–84
Salmon with pebbly mustard sauce, 129
Salsa cruda, 161
Salt. *See* Crook's Corner Cajun Salt

Saturday fish chowder, 165–66
Sauces
    béchamel sauce, 20
    bourbon sauce, 148–49
    cocktail sauce, 119
    Crook's tomato sauce, 120–21
    green sauce, 34
    hot fudge sauce, 140
    lemon sauce, 214–15
    low-fat Cajun sauce, 188
    pebbly mustard sauce, 129
    ravigote sauce, 34–35
    rouille, 35–36
    tartar sauce, 120
    tomato fennel sauce, 13
    tomato sauce, 20
    See also Dessert sauces
Sausage chez vous, 197
Sazerac, 222
Shakespeare sandwiches, 182
Shirley Temple, 222–23
Shortbread, nut, 215–16
Shrimp
    asparagus and shrimp Dijonnaise,
        15–16
    maque choux with shrimp, 130
    shrimp and grits, 130–31
    shrimp-stuffed mirlitons or summer
        squash, 182–83
Sidecar, 223
Slaw. *See* Coleslaw
Sorbets
    blackberry sorbet, 92
    passion fruit sorbet, 92
Soups
    apple celeriac soup, 27
    beet and cucumber soup, 166–67
    carrot soup, 28
    crab soup, 107–8
    cream of onion soup, 29–30

    everyday oyster stew, 164–65
    garlic soup with mushrooms, 108–9
    marmite Provençale, 109
    Mediterranean vegetable soup, 110–11
    mushroom soup forestière, 29
    onion soup Lyonnaise, 30–31
    Oriental mushroom soup, 111
    peanut carrot soup, 168–69
    pumpkin soup, 169–70
    quick black bean soup, 167–68
    Saturday fish chowder, 165–66
    spring soup, 31–32
    vegetable beef soup, 170–71
    white bean soup, 111–12
    winter soup, 32–33
Spinach
    backyard spinach pie, 175–76
    chicken stuffed with spinach and
        cheese, 57–58
    timbale of spinach and mint with fresh
        tomato sauce, 42–43
Spring soup, 31–32
Summer squash. *See* Mirlitons or summer
    squash, shrimp-stuffed
Sweet potatoes
    stuffed sweet potatoes, 124–25
    sweet potato pie, 146–47
Sweetbreads
    sweetbreads écossaise, 70
    sweetbreads with capers and brown
        butter, 69–70

Tartar sauce, 120
Tarte tatin, 76–77
Tarts, jelly, 216–17
Timbales
    broccoli or corn timbales, 38–39
    timbale of spinach and mint with fresh
        tomato sauce, 42–43
Toffee bars, 217–18